UNIVERSITY OF NORTH CAROLINA
STUDIES IN THE ROMANCE LANGUAGES AND LITERATURES
Number 117

HIGHER, HIDDEN ORDER:
DESIGN AND MEANING IN THE ODES OF MALHERBE

HIGHER, HIDDEN ORDER:
DESIGN AND MEANING IN THE ODES OF MALHERBE

BY

DAVID LEE RUBIN

CHAPEL HILL
THE UNIVERSITY OF NORTH CAROLINA PRESS

DEPÓSITO LEGAL: V. 605 - 1972

ARTES GRÁFICAS SOLER, S. A. — JÁVEA, 28 — VALENCIA (8) — 1972

A man's discourse [is] like to a rich Persian carpet, the beautiful figures and patterns of which can only be shown by spreading and extending it out; when it is contracted and folded up, they are obscure and lost.

Plutarch, "Themistocles," 29
(Translated by John Dryden)

In memoriam

JOHN NAPIER
WALTER STIEFEL

ACKNOWLEDGMENTS

Parts of this study have been presented at learned meetings. A draft of Chapter II was read before French Section 1, The Midwest Modern Language Association, Cincinnati, 1968; a summary of Chapter III, before French Section 1, The South Atlantic Modern Language Association, Washington, D. C., 1970; extracts from Chapters I and VIII, before the symposium on baroque lyric poetry at the Third Conference on Seventeenth-Century French Literature, Seattle, 1971.

Two portions have already been published. The second chapter appeared, under the title "Toward A New View of Malherbe: Higher, Hidden Order in the First Completed Ode," in *Poetic Theory/Poetic Practice*, edited by Robert Scholes (Iowa City: M. M. L. A., 1969); the third chapter, under the title "An Intimation of Cancelled Skies: Myth and Image in Malherbe's Second Completed Ode," in *Revue de l'Université d'Ottawa* (January-March, 1971). I am obligated to the copyright owners for permission to reprint these materials with revisions.

For grants-in-aid which provided leisure necessary to the completion of this study and defrayed the cost of typing the manuscript, I wish to thank the Research Committee of the University of Virginia.

I am especially in the debt of Professors Judd D. Hubert, A. H. Pasco, Bruce A. Morrissette, and A. James Arnold, who in conversation or correspondence and by the example of their own critical practice, have stimulated and helped to clarify my own thinking. Finally, I thank my wife Carolyn for her helpfulness and encouragement at every stage of my work.

D. L. R.

Charlottesville, Virginia
April, 1971

CONTENTS

Pages

	Acknowledgments	11
I.	From Unity to Coherence	15
II.	Breaking the Circle	22
III.	A Glimpse into Chaos	37
IV.	The Poetics of Grandeur	51
V.	The Gemini	68
VI.	The Idea of Order	83
VII.	The First Subject of the Realm	94
VIII.	From Coherence to Judgment	108
	Appendix: "Si quelque avorton..."	113
	Selective Bibliography	123

I

FROM UNITY TO COHERENCE

Critics and historians of seventeenth-century French literature agree that the odes of François de Malherbe are the major work of a pre-eminent poet. There is far less consensus, however, about the grounds for ascribing esthetic value to these poems.
The traditional view — enunciated at the Sorbonne — emphasizes the odes' conformity to the norms of deductive logic. For Gustave Lanson, it is an "impersonnelle démonstration" which distinguishes the odes.[1] Raymond Lebègue sees in them a "composition rigoureuse," which is to say a "discours logique et oratoire d'où les digressions sont bannies... et où les articulations sont saillantes."[2]
"Such comments, we shall see, have little to justify them," wrote Professor Philip A. Wadsworth at the beginning of his important article, "Form and Content in the Odes of Malherbe."[3] To discredit the conventional wisdom, Professor Wadsworth analyzed the order and articulation of themes in each of the poems. His analyses showed that:

> a forceful argument, in Malherbe, is not necessarily a logical one. Some of his odes contain material which can be eliminated... some have a rather loose structure with little continuity from theme to theme, some depart widely from the principal subject. Malherbe was a master of form

---

[1] *Histoire de la littérature française* (Paris: Hachette, 1912), p. 359.
[2] *La Poésie française de 1560 à 1630* (Paris: Société d'Edition d'Ensignement Supérieur, 1951), II, pp. 84-85.
[3] *P. M. L. A.*, 78 (June, 1963), p. 190.

in individual lines and stanzas, but the form or coherence of a whole poem seemed less important to him.[4]

Malherbe's apparent indifference to exposition in his longer poems led Professor Wadsworth to a double conclusion. First,

> Malherbe bears the stamp of the age he lived in, an age whose sensibility is nowadays often described as baroque. What we have brought to light in his poetry can be found in that of many other French writers of the early seventeenth century, such as Régnier, Théophile de Viau, Saint-Amant, and Tristan l'Hermite. In their longer poems — whether ode, satire, elegy, or epistle — they wrote in a rather haphazard, accumulative manner, with little concern for structural unity.[5]

Secondly, Professor Wadsworth drew attention to the prescriptive Renaissance theory of the ode:

> elle se donne les apparences du désordre dans les successions de faits et les liaisons d'expressions.... Mais ce désordre n'est qu'un ordre supérieur et caché.[6]

On this basis, it follows that by neglect of logic, Malherbe achieved "le beau désordre," but it would be "harder to prove [that] he ... attained 'un ordre supérieur et caché.'"[7]

The implication is plain: the absence of logical unity in Malherbe's odes — coupled with an apparent lack of evidence for some other structuring technique — may signal not merely the odes' generic faultiness, but above all their lack of value as literary artifacts, considered *in vacuo*.

Despite this scepticism — expressed and implied — Professor Wadsworth opened another new perspective on the odes when, in the same article, he observed that "it is not easy to separate this aspect [i. e., the arrangement of themes in] ... the poems from the many others which contribute to their poetic structure,

---

[4] Wadsworth, p. 194.
[5] *Ibid.*
[6] René Bray, *La Formation de la doctrine classique en France*, 2nd ed. (Paris: Nizet, 1957), pp. 352-353. Cited by Professor Wadsworth, p. 195.
[7] Wadsworth, p. 195.

such as imagery, harmonic qualities, feelings, rhymes, and vocabulary." [8]

Indeed, a synthetic study of the odes may show that they possess a "higher, hidden order" attributable less to the logical unity for which Professor Wadsworth analyzed them than to the organic coherence of wholes, whose plot and character, argumentation and style converge on one or several related thematic centers. It is this possibility that the present work will explore.

* * *

The principal means by which poets of the sixteenth and seventeenth centuries integrated their creations is the prolonged comparison. But, according to Jean Rousset, to propose this technique as the source of "higher, hidden order" in Malherbe's odes would be a serious error:

> A trente ans, le Malherbe des *Larmes de Saint Pierre,* loin d'éviter les métaphores, les fait proliférer, les cultive et surtout les prolonge.... Il est visible qu'à ce moment-là Malherbe ne craint pas la métaphore prolongée. Et le Malherbe de la maturité, après 1600? On connaît son attitude de principe: il les marque fréquemment d'infamie chez Desportes quand elles sont prolongées; il les ridiculise chez tel de ses disciples; de fait, il passe pour en être l'ennemi.... Mais quelle est sa pratique?.... Ce qui disparaît entièrement après 1600, ce sont les métaphores prolongées, c'est l'image s'engendrant à partir de l'image, au défi de la censure logique. Et ce qui disparaît également, c'est le mouvement générateur accordé à l'image, c'est la métaphore organisant activement le poème et se propageant au delà de la strophe. La métaphore malherbienne, quand elle paraît, demeure subordonnée au sein de la strophe, immobilisée, stérilisée, et toujours soumise à l'édifice. La poésie a cessé d'être aux yeux de Malherbe, création de métaphores originales et vivantes. [9]

Though almost certainly true for the *explicit* comparison (the most pervasive class), Professor Rousset's observation invites discussion

---

[8] Wadsworth, p. 194.
[9] "La Poésie au temps de Malherbe: la métaphore," *Dix-septième siècle,* No. 31 (April, 1956), p. 362.

when extended to the *implicit* comparison. The presence of the latter in seventeenth-century French literature is well-attested, though until this study, not in works written before 1643 — fifteen years after Malherbe's death.

An explicit comparison is that which occurs in a poem like the thirtieth sonnet of Du Bellay's *Antiquités de Rome:*

>   Comme le champ semé en verdure foisonne,
>   De verdure se haulse en tuyau verdissant,
>   Du tuyau se herisse en epic florissant,
>   D'epic jaunit en grain que le chauld assaisonne;
>   5   Et comme en la saison le rustique moissonne
>   Les undoyans cheveux du sillon blondissant,
>   Les met d'ordre en javelle, & du blé jaunissant
>   Sur le champ despouillé mille gerbes façonne:
>   Ainsi de peu à peu creut l'Empire Romain,
>   10   Tant qu'il fut despouillé par la Barbare main,
>   Qui ne laissa de luy que ces marques antiques,
>   Que chacun va pillant: comme on void le gleneur
>   Cheminant pas à pas recueillir les reliques
>   De ce qui va tumbant apres le moissonneur. [10]

Du Bellay constructed this sonnet on a proportional analogy, according to which growth and harvest are to a field of wheat what rise to power and pillage were to ancient Rome. If the poet had chosen to intensify the lofty pathos of his speaker's tone, he might have replaced the "comme" and "ainsi" by such formulas as would fully identify the terms with one another, thus creating a metaphor instead of a simile. Such a change, however, would not have altered the basic structure. This structure — an explicit comparison — formally asserts likeness or identity and elaborates the assertion without permitting fusion of principal and secondary terms. It is this type of comparison that Malherbe ridiculed and after 1600 did not employ as a principle of large-scale composition in his major poems. But what of the implicit comparison, such as that contained in the following fable of Jean de la Fontaine?

* * *

---

[10] *Les Regrets et autres œuvres poétiques*, eds. J. Joliffe and M. A. Screech (Geneva: Droz, 1966), p. 304.

LA TORTUË ET LES DEUX CANARDS

Une Tortuë estoit, à la teste legere,
Qui lasse de son trou voulut voir le pays,
Volontiers on fait cas d'une terre étrangere:
Volontiers gens boiteux haïssent le logis.
5   Deux Canards à qui la Commere
       Communiqua ce beau dessein
Luy dirent qu'ils avoient dequoy la satisfaire:
       Voyez-vous ce large chemin?
Nous vous voiturerons par l'air en Amerique,
10   Vous verrez mainte Republique,
Maint Royaume, maint peuple, et vous profiterez
Des differentes mœurs que vous remarquerez.
Ulysse en fit autant. On ne s'attendoit guere
       De voir Ulysse en cette affaire.
15 La Tortuë écouta la proposition.
Marché fait, les oiseaux forgent une machine
       Pour transporter la pelerine.
Dans la gueule en travers on luy passe un baston.
Serrez bien, dirent-ils; gardez de lascher prise:
20 Puis chaque Canard prend ce baston par un bout.
La Tortuë enlevée on s'étonne partout
       De voir aller en cette guise
       L'animal lent et sa maison,
Justement au milieu de l'un et l'autre Oison.
25 Miracle, crioit-on. Venez voir dans les nuës
       Passer la Reine des Tortuës.
—La Reine. Vrayment ouy. Je la suis en effet;
Ne vous en moquez point. Elle eût beaucoup mieux fait
De passer son chemin sans dire aucune chose;
30 Car laschant le baston en desserrant les dents,
Elle tombe, elle creve aux pieds des regardans.
Son indiscretion de sa perte fut cause.
Imprudence, babil, et sotte vanité,
       Et vaine curiosité,

35   Ont ensemble estroit parentage;
        Ce sont enfans tous d'un lignage.
                                (X, 2) [11]

* * *

An obvious resemblance exists between the turtle and a certain type of human fool. But embedded within that resemblance there are two covert analogies which invest the poem with ironic sense and in so doing assure its coherence. First, in plot, character, and thought, the fable ironically inverts the motifs of Homer's *Odyssey*. Whereas Ulysses leaves a foreign land to regain his home, and during the long, circuitous voyage survives one danger after another because of his cunning, the turtle leaves home merely to see the world, and scarcely embarks before her egregious stupidity and imprudence cause her premature death. Indeed, "On ne s'attendoit guere / De voir Ulysse en cette affaire." The poet further develops his central idea on the stylistic level, where he likens the turtle's mind and fate to a void. The turtle has a "teste legere" (v. 1) — the adjective taken here in its psychological sense of "inconstant" or "unreflective," but also in its material sense of "lightweight." The reason for this lightness is "sotte vanité, / Et vaine curiosité" (vv. 33 and 34) — the key words are also taken doubly: in their usual sense, which refers to pride and futility, and in their etymological sense, which refers to emptiness. The turtle's mind is vacuous, hence she embarks on a senseless journey, at the very beginning of which she is so full only of herself (which is to say, nothing), that she forgets her limitations and falls to earth. It is crucial that "elle creve" (v. 31) at the spectators' feet. "Crever" means not only to die but to burst, and upon bursting, a turtle's shell releases its contents and becomes empty. The turtle thus suffers punishment in the image of her defect: for vacuousness, she becomes a void. This system of elements — words and motifs which, taken literally, advance the lyric, dramatic, narrative, and rhetorical development of the text, but which, taken figuratively imply the secondary terms of thematically significant analogies —

---

[11] *Fables choisies et mises en vers*, 2 vols., ed. Ferdinand Gohin. (Paris: Société Les Belles Lettres, 1934), II, pp. 156-157.

is the implicit comparison. That in their dramatic works Corneille, Rotrou, Molière, and Racine exploited the implicit comparison has been amply demonstrated by Professor Judd D. Hubert.[12] But just as Malherbe was silent on the admissibility of this technique, his critics have yet to make their pronouncement about his use or avoidance of it in the major poems of his maturity.

* * *

The lacuna just described furnishes additional motivation for this study, whose object is to examine anew the odes of François de Malherbe. Following — with one exception — the order of the odes' composition, the next six chapters each treat one ode; included are a summary of the historical circumstances necessary to its comprehension, the complete definitive text, Professor Wadsworth's critique, and a new reading designed to ascertain if the ode achieves coherence by use of implicit comparison. The last chapter offers a definition of the malherbian ode as a structural system and traces its development from 1600 to 1628. Finally, the appendix presents a new case, founded on internal evidence, for the incompleteness of Malherbe's ode of 1614.

---

[12] *Essai d'exégèse racinienne* (Paris: Nizet, 1956) and *Molière and the Comedy of the Intellect* (Berkeley and Los Angeles: University of California Press, 1962). Stephen C. Pepper has explained the philosophical assumptions of this critical view in two books, *World Hypotheses* (Berkeley: The University of California Press, 1942), pp. 280-314, and *The Basis of Criticism in the Arts* (Cambridge: Harvard University Press, 1945), pp. 74-95. Critical manifestos setting forth the position include *Theory of Literature*, by René Wellek and Austin Warren (New York: Harcourt, Brace, 1949) and *The Verbal Icon*, by William K. Wimsatt (Lexington: University of Kentucky Press, 1954). Among the best examples of this method in its application to English poetry is *The Well-Wrought Urn*, by Cleanth Brooks (New York: Harcourt, Brace, 1947). Professor A. H. Pasco has carried this method very far toward the solution of problems posed by the metaphorical use of allusion; see his "Marcel, Albertine and Balbec in Proust's Allusive Complex," *Romanic Review* 62 (1971), 113-126.

II

BREAKING THE CIRCLE

Marie de Médicis and Henri IV, King of France, were married by proxy in Florence on October 5, 1600. Eight days later, the bride sailed for Marseille, landing there on November 3, and departing for the north on the 16th. She arrived early the next afternoon at Aix-en-Provence, where attended by Bellegarde and Guise she received the homage of local dignitaries and authors, including François de Malherbe, who presented her with his first completed ode.[1]

* * *

A LA REINE SUR SA

BIEN-VENUE EN FRANCE

I   Peuples, qu'on mette sur la teste
    Tout ce que la terre a de fleurs:
    Peuples, que ceste belle feste
    A jamais tarisse nos pleurs:
    Qu'aux deux bous du monde se voye   5
    Luire le feu de nostre joye:
    Et soient dans les coupes noyez

---

[1] François de Malherbe, *Œuvres poétiques*, eds. René Fromilhague and Raymond Lebègue, 2 vols. (Paris: Société Les Belles Lettres, 1968), II, p. 26.

Les soucis de tous ces orages,
Que pour nos rebelles courages
Les Dieux nous avoient envoyez.   10

II   A ce coup iront en fumee
Les vœux que faisoient nos mutins,
En leur Ame encor affamee
De massacres et de butins:
Nos doutes seront esclaircies: 15
Et mentiront les Propheties
De tous ces visages pallis,
Dont le vain estude s'applique
A chercher l'an climaterique
De l'eternelle Fleur de lys.   20

III Aujourd'huy nous est amenee
Cette Princesse que la foy
D'Amour ensemble et d'Hymenee
Destine au lict de nostre Roy:
La voicy la belle Marie,   25
Belle merveille d'Hetrurie,
Qui faict confesser au Soleil,
Quoy que l'âge passé raconte,
Que du Ciel depuis qu'il y monte,
Ne vint jamais rien de pareil.   30

IV   Telle n'est point la Cytheree,
Quand d'un nouveau feu s'allumant,
Elle sort pompeuse et paree
Pour la conqueste d'un Amant:
Telle ne luit en sa carriere   35
Des mois l'inegale courriere:
Et telle dessus l'Orizon
L'Aurore au matin ne s'estale,
Quand les yeux mesmes de Cefale
En feroient la comparaison.   40

V   Le Sceptre que porte sa race,
Où l'heur aux merites est joint,

Luy met le respect en la face,
Mais il ne l'enorgueillit point:
Nulle vanité ne la touche: 45
Les Graces parlent par sa bouche:
Et son front tesmoin asseuré
Qu'au vice elle est inaccessible,
Ne peut que d'un cœur insensible
Estre veu sans estre adoré. 50

VI Quantesfois lors que sur les ondes,
Ce nouveau miracle flottoit,
Neptune en ses caves profondes
Plaignit-il le feu qu'il sentoit?
Et quantesfois en sa pensee 55
De vives attaintes blessee,
Sans l'honneur de la Royauté
Qui luy fit celer son martyre,
Eust-il voulu de son Empire
Faire eschange à ceste Beauté? 60

VII Dix jours ne pouvant se distraire
Du plaisir de la regarder,
Il a par un effort contraire
Essayé de la retarder:
Mais à la fin, soit que l'audace, 65
Au meilleur advis ait fait place,
Soit qu'un autre Demon plus fort,
Aux vents ait imposé silence,
Elle est hors de sa violence,
Et la voicy dans nostre port. 70

VIII La voicy, Peuples, qui nous montre
Tout ce que la gloire a de pris:
Les fleurs naissent à sa rencontre
Dans les cœurs, et dans les esprits:
Et la presence des merveilles 75
Qu'en oyoient dire nos oreilles,
Accuse la temerité
De ceux qui nous l'avoient décrite,

D'avoir figuré son merite
Moindre que n'est la verité. 80

IX O toute parfaite Princesse,
L'estonnement de l'Univers,
Astre par qui vont avoir cesse
Nos tenebres, et nos hyvers:
Exemple sans autres exemples, 85
Future Image de nos temples,
Quoy que nostre foible pouvoir
En vostre accueil ose entreprendre,
Peut il esperer de vous rendre
Ce que nous vous allons devoir? 90

X Ce sera vous qui de nos villes
Ferez la beauté refleurir,
Vous, qui de nos haines civiles
Ferez la racine mourir:
Et par vous la paix asseuree 95
N'aura pas la courte duree
Qu'esperent infidellement,
Non lassez de nostre souffrance,
Ces François qui n'ont de la France,
Que la langue et l'habillement. 100

XI Par vous un Dauphin nous va naistre,
Que vous mesmes verrez un jour
De la terre entiere le maistre,
Ou par armes ou par amour:
Et ne tarderont ses conquestes 105
Dans les Oracles desja prestes,
Qu'autant que le premier coton,
Qui de jeunesse est le message,
Tardera d'estre en son visage,
Et de faire ombre à son menton. 110

XII O combien lors aura de veuves
La gent qui porte le Turban!
Que de sang rougira les fleuves

Qui lavent les pieds du Liban!
Que le Bosfore en ses deux rives 115
Aura de Sultanes captives!
Et que de meres à Memfis,
En pleurant diront la vaillance
De son courage et de sa lance,
Aux funerailles de leurs fils! 120

XIII Cependant nostre grand Alcide,
Amolly parmy vos appas,
Perdra la fureur qui sans bride
L'emporte à chercher le trespas:
Et ceste valeur indontee 125
De qui l'honneur est l'Euristee,
Puis que rien n'a sçeu l'obliger
A ne nous donner plus d'alarmes,
Au moins pour espargner vos larmes
Aura peur de nous affliger. 130

XIV Si l'espoir qu'aux bouches des hommes
Nos beaux faits seront recitez,
Est l'aiguillon par qui nous sommes
Dans les hazards precipitez:
Luy de qui la gloire semee 135
Par les voix de la renommee
En tant de parts s'est fait ouyr,
Que tout le siecle en est un livre,
N'est-il pas indigne de vivre
S'il ne vit pour se resjouyr? 140

XV Qu'il luy suffise que l'Espagne
Reduitte par tant de combas
A ne l'oser voir en campagne,
A mis l'ire, et les armes bas:
Qu'il ne provoque point l'envie 145
Du mauvais sort contre sa vie:
Et puis que selon son dessein
Il a rendu nos troubles calmes,

S'il veut d'avantage de palmes,
Qu'il les aquere en vostre sein. 150

XVI   C'est là qu'il faut qu'à son Genie,
Seul arbitre de ses plaisirs,
Quoy qu'il demande il ne denie
Rien qu'imaginent ses desirs:
C'est là qu'il faut que les annees 155
Luy coulent comme des journees
Et qu'il ait dequoy se vanter,
Que la douceur qui tout excede,
N'est point ce que sert Ganimede
A la table de Jupiter. 160

XVII   Mais d'aller plus à ces batailles,
Où tonnent les foudres d'enfer,
Et lutter contre des murailles,
D'où pleuvent la flamme et le fer,
Puis qu'il sçait qu'en ses destinees 165
Les nostres seront terminees,
Et qu'apres luy nostre discord
N'aura plus qui domte sa rage,
N'est-ce pas nous rendre au naufrage
Apres nous avoir mis à bord? 170

XVIII   Cét Achile de qui la pique
Faisoit aux braves d'Ilion
La terreur que fait en Affrique
Aux troupeaux l'assaut d'un Lyon,
Bien que sa mere eust à ses armes, 175
Adjousté la force des charmes,
Quand les Destins l'eurent permis,
N'eut-il pas sa trame coupee,
De la moins redoutable espee
Qui fust parmy ses ennemis? 180

XIX   Les Parques d'une mesme soye
Ne devident pas tous nos jours:

Ny tousjours par semblable voye
Ne font les planettes leur cours:
Quoy que promette la Fortune, 185
A la fin quand on l'importune,
Ce qu'elle avoit fait prosperer
Tombe du feste au precipice:
Et pour l'avoir tousjours propice
Il la faut tousjours reverer. 190

XX Je sçay bien que sa Carmagnole
Devant luy se representant,
Telle qu'une plaintive Idole
Va son courroux sollicitant,
Et l'invite à prendre pour elle 195
Une legitime querelle:
Mais doit-il vouloir que pour luy
Nous ayons tousjours le teint blesme,
Cependant qu'il tente luy-mesme
Ce qu'il peut faire par autruy? 200

XXI Si vos yeux sont toute sa braise,
Et vous la fin de tous ses vœux,
Peut-il pas languir à son aise
En la prison de vos cheveux?
Et commettre aux dures corvees 205
Toutes ces Ames relevees,
Que d'un conseil ambitieux
La faim de gloire persuade
D'aller sur les pas d'Encelade
Porter des escheles aux Cieux? 210

XXII Apollon n'a point de mistere,
Et sont profanes ses chansons,
Ou devant que le Sagitere,
Deux fois rameine les glaçons,
Le succez de leurs entreprises, 215
De qui deux Provinces conquises
Ont desja fait preuve à leur dan,
Favorisé de la victoire,

Changera la fable en histoire
De Phaëton en l'Eridan. 220

XXIII Nice payant avecques honte
Un siege autrefois repoussé,
Cessera de nous mettre en conte
Barberousse qu'elle a chassé:
Guise en ses murailles forcees, 225
Remettra les bornes passees,
Qu'avoit nostre Empire marin:
Et Soissons fatal aux superbes,
Fera chercher parmy les herbes,
En quelle place fut Turin.² 230

* * *

Before entering into the commentary, let us consider the difficulties uncovered by logical analysis of this ode. Witness the themes and their progression in Professor Wadsworth's résumé:

> Stanzas 1-2. Invitation for the people to rejoice and to forget past misfortunes. 3-5. Praise for the beauty and virtue of Marie. 6-7. Her voyage from Italy; Neptune fell in love with her and detained her ten days. 8-10. Praise for her perfection; prediction that she will bring peace to France. 11-12. This royal marriage will lead to the birth of a prince, a great conquerer. 13-21. In honor of the King: may the pleasures of love keep Henri IV at home so that he will not continue to risk his life on the battlefield. 22-23. France's recent and forthcoming military victories, under the leadership of various great noblemen.³

Professor Wadsworth's analysis is followed by a series of disquieting questions and observations:

> To what extent does Malherbe attempt to weave his themes into a homogeneous pattern or a connected discourse? Readers will find that certain stanzas are virtually detachable; they can be suppressed without this seeming

---

² Malherbe, I, pp. 80-87.
³ Wadsworth, p. 191.

> to harm the poem — not only the Neptune incident but also the two concluding stanzas with their allusions to particular campaigns and generals.... What exactly was the poet's concept of good poetic form? One suspects that we are dealing with a type of verse in which rigorous logical structure is not important, a type of verse built around a cluster of themes, all related to one another but not closely interdependent.[4]

A solution to these perplexities may be found on a level of structure less involved with deductive reasoning than with allusion.

The parallels that the poet draws between his subjects and certain mythological personages are of special interest. To be sure many of these comparisons belong to the repertory of conventional praise; but on close examination, they appear not only to embellish and elevate the principals, but above all to evoke a specific mythological pattern which underlies and lends meaning to the poem's literal action.

In the portraiture, for example, there is convergence in the selection and deployment of features. Marie de Médicis is nothing less than a divinity:

> La voicy la belle Marie,
> Belle merveille d'Hetrurie,
> Qui faict confesser au Soleil,
> Quoy que l'âge passé raconte,
> Que du Ciel depuis qu'il y monte,
> Ne vint jamais rien de pareil.   (vv. 25-30)

Since, in the seventeenth century, the word "merveille" denoted not only *marvel* but also *miracle*, Malherbe here attributes to the Queen a supernatural character and origin just as he will later charge her with a redemptive mission. A few stanzas below, Malherbe will repeat this attribution, stating that the Queen, in transit from Italy, is "ce nouveau miracle" (v. 52). As such, she surpasses Venus and Aurora in splendor (vv. 31-40); moreover, because of her flawless grace and character, her countenance cannot "estre veu sans estre adoré" (v. 50). Malherbe completes this picture by a prediction found in the ninth stanza, that Marie

---
[4] *Ibid.*

de Médicis is the "Future Image de nos temples" (v. 86). It is difficult to identify the goddess whom the Queen resembles. At one point, she parallels Athena or other patronesses of cities: addressing the Queen, the poet defines part of her earthly mission in the following terms: "Ce sera vous qui de nos villes / Ferez la beauté refleurir" (vv. 91-92). Elsewhere, Venus seems in the ascendant, not only by the suggestion of amorous delights awaiting the King, but in particular because "Les fleurs naissent à sa rencontre / Dans les cœurs, et dans les esprits" (vv. 73-74). In its material form, this effect signals the Cyprian's presence.

If Malherbe's portrait of Marie de Médicis seems somewhat indirect, nothing could be more explicit than his comparison of Henri IV to a mythological hero. Needing no introduction to contemporary readers, the King appears quite simply as the greatest warrior of them all, "nostre grand Alcide" (v. 121), Hercules himself.

Finally, the son of this royal couple will inherit special qualities from both parents. His military virtues, like his father's, will inspire woe and wonder wherever he does battle: "Et que de meres à Memfis, / En pleurant diront la vaillance / De son courage et de sa lance" (vv. 117-119). He will also exercise a power over the affections, thus becoming "De la terre entiere le maistre, / Ou par armes ou par amour" (vv. 103-104). Since the Queen resembles Venus, Malherbe has apparently drawn a circumspect parallel between the Dauphin and Aeneas, who — armed with his mother's ability to fascinate the opposite sex — won Lavinia as a first step toward gaining control of Latium.

The complex of portraits and relationships just described recalls myths which figure in the background of *The Iliad* and *The Odyssey* and which appear in Books XI and XIII of Ovid's *Metamorphoses*. In the first case, the sea nymph Thetis married Peleus, a participant in the Calydonian Hunt; their son was Achilles. In the second case, Venus had a liaison with Anchises, prince of Dardanus, and bore his son, Aeneas. The common denominator of both myths and of the present ode is the following system of motifs: the union of goddess or demigoddess with hero or prince, and the birth of a son destined to become a great hero. In addition to these, there appears a third motif: the couple's separation caused by male pride. Peleus, prematurely jealous of his son's fame as a warrior, attempted to obstruct his wife's effort to render Achilles invulnerable. Thetis therefore deserted her husband. Anchises, for his part, boasted in public that he had enjoyed the favors of a goddess, and infuriated, Venus struck him blind. It is precisely to this motif of separation that Malherbe devotes the four stanzas disqualified by logical analysis as superfluous.

The first pair of dizains relates the Neptune incident.

> Quantesfois lors que sur les ondes,
> Ce nouveau miracle flottoit,
> Neptune en ses caves profondes
> Plaignit-il le feu qu'il sentoit?
> Et quantesfois en sa pensee
> De vives attaintes blessee,
> Sans l'honneur de la Royauté
> Qui luy fit celer son martyre,
> Eust-il voulu de son Empire
> Faire eschange à ceste Beauté?
>
> Dix jours ne pouvant se distraire
> Du plaisir de la regarder,
> Il a par un effort contraire
> Essayé de la retarder:
> Mais à la fin, soit que l'audace,
> Au meilleur advis ait fait place,
> Soit qu'un autre Demon plus fort,
> Aux vents ait imposé le silence,
> Elle est hors de sa violence,
> Et la voicy dans nostre port. (vv. 51-70)

These lines, in themselves, do not contain the separation motif proper, to be developed later. The short-lived event narrated here precedes the first meeting of Marie de Médicis and her husband; it is not caused by the King's pride; and Marie de Médicis does not surrender to her admirer. But the account *does* perform other important functions. Superficially, it confirms the poet's praise for the royal bride: although Marie is so irresistibly beautiful that Neptune might have renounced the sea to possess her, she is too noble to desert Henri IV and unite adulterously, even with another divinity. That the episode prepares for the separation motif proper is more striking. Clearly, even if the union enjoys the somewhat ambiguous auspices of one supernatural power — "un autre Demon plus fort" — still others, like Neptune, may seek to interfere with the marriage or even threaten its destruction. This point is crucial to what follows.

The apparently unnecessary references to specific campaigns and generals at the end of the poem play an important role in the poet's treatment of possible separation. But to grasp the full meaning requires discussion of the entire context.

In respect to character, the King is superhuman. He brings to the battlefield a "fureur qui sans bride / L'emporte à chercher le trespas" (vv. 123-124). This ferocity, linked with an almost insatiable ambition, is not far removed from hybris and hence it unsettles the poet, who exclaims "Qu'il ne provoque point l'envie / Du mauvais sort contre sa vie" (vv. 145-146). Like another great warrior, the King runs the risk of humiliation by destiny or fortune:

> Cét Achile, de qui la pique
> Faisoit aux braves d'Ilion
> La terreur que fait en Affrique
> Aux troupeaux l'assaut d'un Lyon,
> Bien que sa mere eust à ses armes,
> Adjousté la force des charmes,
> Quand les Destins l'eurent permis,
> N'eut-il pas sa trame coupee,
> De la moins redoutable espee
> Qui fust parmi ses ennemis?
>
> Les Parques d'une mesme soye
> Ne devident pas tous nos jours:
> Ny tousjours par semblable voye
> Ne font les planettes leurs cours:
> Quoy que promette la Fortune,
> À la fin quand on l'importune,
> Ce qu'elle avoit fait prosperer
> Tombe du feste au precipice:
> Et pour l'avoir tousjours propice
> Il la faut tousjours reverer. (vv. 171-190)

Indeed, should Henri IV return to battle, not only will he endanger his own life, but he will also put the interests of France into jeopardy:

> Puis qu'il sçait qu'en ses destinees
> Les nostres seront terminees,
> Et qu'apres luy nostre discord
> N'aura plus qui domte sa rage,
> N'est-ce pas nous rendre au naufrage
> Apres nous avoir mis à bord?   (vv. 165-170)

Thus has Malherbe given the separation motif a new variant: as in the case of the mythological couples, the marriage of this goddess and hero may end — and, incidentally, all hope for the recovery of the hero's nation — if, in his pride, the hero again tempts fate to destroy him, however praiseworthy may be his actions.

An accompanying series of questions and exhortations, addressed mainly to the Queen, prescribes a manner by which the royal couple may avert disaster. First and most importantly, Marie must domesticate Henri IV:

> Et qu'il ait dequoy se vanter,
> Que la douceur que tout excede,
> N'est point ce que sert Ganimede
> A la table de Jupiter.   (vv. 157-160)

To accomplish this, she must captivate the hero's heart:

> Si vos yeux sont toute sa braise,
> Et vous la fin de tous ses voeux,
> Peut-il pas languir à son aise
> En la prison de vos cheveux?   (vv. 201-204)

She must transform into gallantry his craving for military success:

> S'il veut d'avantage de palmes,
> Qu'il les aquere en vostre sein.   (vv. 149-150)

And if his love becomes all consuming, he may hesitate to participate directly in war:

> Au moins pour espargner vos larmes
> [Il] aura peur de nous affliger.   (vv. 129-130)

Finally, the King must delegate his military responsibilities:

> Mais doit-il vouloir que pour luy
> Nous ayons tousjours le teint blesme,

> Cependant qu'il tente luy-mesme
> Ce qu'il peut faire par autruy? (vv. 197-200)

Turning now to the second pair of doubtful stanzas, one may test their necessity by supposing the poem's effectiveness if Malherbe had indeed chosen not to include them. Bearing in mind the poet's evocation of hope and fear for the well-being of France, the reader recognizes that while national reconstruction is fostered by the divine Marie, it depends wholly on the King's willingness to retire from direct participation in war. To counterbalance the King's overzealous character, however, Malherbe has so far offered only questions and exhortations, none of which opens a very convincing perspective on Henri IV's renunciation of arms. In fact, were the poem to end at this point, nothing would prevent the King, the Queen, or the people (to whom this ode is jointly addressed) from inferring that circumstances foreign or domestic would almost certainly oblige the King to return to the battlefield and suffer the punishment of fate, thus prematurely ending his marriage and bringing catastrophe to France. Lest the rhetoric fail the poet must change his mode of discourse. The way is prepared for the final stanzas:

> Apollon n'a point de mistere,
> Et sont profanes ses chansons,
> Ou devant que le Sagitere,
> Deux fois rameine les glaçons,
> Les succez de leurs entreprises,
> De qui deux Provinces conquises
> Ont desja fait preuve à leur dan,
> Favorisé de la victoire,
> Changera la fable en histoire
> De Phaëton en l'Eridan.
>
> Nice, payant avecques honte
> Un siege autrefois repoussé,
> Cessera de nous mettre en conte
> Barberousse qu'elle a chassé:
> Guise en ses murailles forcees,
> Remettra les bornes passees,
> Qu'avoit nostre empire marin:
> Et Soissons fatal aux superbes,
> Fera chercher parmi les herbes,
> En quelle place fut Turin. (vv. 211-230)

Malherbe has abruptly shifted from long-term prediction to fact and imminent fact. Under the leadership of Biron, Crillon, and Lesdiguières, Bresse and Savoy have fallen to French forces. That Henri IV had set this region high on his list of military priorities is evident from an earlier passage, where Malherbe contemplates what may lure the King into danger:

> Je sçay bien que sa Carmagnole
> Devant luy se representant,
> Telle qu'une plaintive Idole
> Va son courroux sollicitant,
> Et l'invite à prendre pour elle
> Une legitime querelle.   (vv. 191-196)

Given the fall of Bresse and Savoy, it is not unreasonable to forsee the immediate conquest of Nice, part of the same duchy, and of Turin, its capital. But Malherbe does more than reel off facile prophecies. He confides the last of these victories to Guise and Soissons, the former a Catholic, the latter a Protestant, and both previously engaged at various times in opposition to the rule of Henri IV. In one stroke, Malherbe demonstrates that others may successfully pursue the King's foreign military objectives, thus answering the question posed in verses 196-200, and he suggests that the King need not fear internal strife, since old rivals, now reconciled to the crown, successfully execute its external policies. By shifting from the desirable to the actual and the impending, Malherbe proves that Henri IV should no longer hesitate: his retirement from the battlefield is now as feasible as it is expedient.

The larger sense of the foregoing is abundantly clear. If the King decides to renounce direct participation in war, he and his Queen will break the tragic circle of pride and separation that trapped their legendary predecessors. Moreover, by so doing they will transform themselves into personages uniquely worthy of veneration by contemporaries and by posterity. Indeed, they will become the principals of a new and felicitous model for relations among those who, superior in kind and degree to ordinary men, control the destiny of nations.

III

A GLIMPSE INTO CHAOS

Malherbe's second completed ode — which occupied him throughout the year 1606 — makes extended reference to a minor historical event which has survived in the recollections of Claude L'Estoile:

> Comme le Roy revenant de la chasse, passoit à cheval sur le Pont-Neuf, environ les cinq heures du soir, se rencontra un fou, qui, ayant ung poingnard nud sous son manteau, tascha d'en offenser Sa Majesté; et l'ayant saisi par le derrière de son manteau, que le Roy avoit agraphé, le secoua assez longtemps jusques à ce que chacun estant accouru au secours, estant pris et interrogé sur ce qu'il vouloit faire, dit qu'il vouloit tuer le Roy, pource qu'il lui détenoit injustement son bien et la pluspart de son Roiaume, et plusieurs autres folies; puis, en riant, dit que pour le moins, il lui avait fait belle peur. Ce fol s'appeloit Jacques des Isles, natif de Senlis, practicien et procureur dudit lieu, et transporté dès-longtemps de son esprit.[1]

* * *

---

[1] Malherbe, II, pp. 20-21.

SUR L'ATTENTAT COMMIS EN LA PERSONNE DE SA MAJESTÉ, LE 19 DE DECEMBRE 1605

I   Que direz-vous races futures
Si quelquefois un vray discours
Vous recite les avantures
De nos abominables jours:
Lirez-vous sans rougir de honte,   5
Que nostre impieté surmonte,
Les faits les plus audacieux,
Et les plus dignes du tonnerre,
Qui firent jamais à la terre,
Sentir la colere des Cieux.   10

II   O que nos fortunes prosperes
Ont un change bien apparent!
O que du siecle de nos Peres
Le nostre s'est faict different:
La France devant ces orages   15
Pleine de meurs, et de courages,
Qu'on ne pouvoit assez loüer,
S'est faict aujourd'huy si tragique,
Qu'elle produit ce que l'Affrique
Auroit vergongne d'avoüer.   20

III   Quelles preuves incomparables
Peut donner un Prince de soy,
Que les Roys les plus adorables
N'en quittent l'honneur à mon Roy?
Quelle terre n'est parfumee   25
Des odeurs de sa renommee?
Et qui peut nier qu'apres Dieu,
Sa gloire qui n'a point d'exemples,
N'ait merité que dans nos temples
On luy donne le second lieu?   30

IV   Qui ne sçait point qu'à sa vaillance
     Il ne se peut rien adjouster?
     Qu'on reçoit de sa bien-vueillance,
     Tout ce qu'on en doit souhaitter?
     Et que si de ceste Couronne,   35
     Que sa tige Illustre luy donne,
     Les Loix ne l'eussent revestu,
     Nos peuples d'un juste suffrage
     Ne pouvoient sans faire naufrage
     Ne l'offrir point à sa vertu?   40

V   Toutesfois ingrats que nous sommes,
     Barbares et desnaturez,
     Plus qu'en ce climat où les hommes
     Par les hommes sont devorez:
     Tousjours nous assaillons sa teste   45
     De quelque nouvelle tempeste:
     Et d'un courage forcené,
     Rejettant son obeïssance,
     Luy deffendons la jouyssance
     Du repos qu'il nous a donné.   50

VI   La main de cet esprit farouche,
     Qui sorty des ombres d'Enfer,
     D'un coup sanglant frappa sa bouche,
     A peine avoit laissé le fer:
     Et voicy qu'un autre perfide,   55
     Où la mesme audace reside,
     Comme si destruire l'Estat
     Tenoit lieu de juste conqueste,
     De pareilles armes s'appreste
     A faire un pareil attentat.   60

VII O Soleil, ô grand luminaire,
     Si jadis l'horreur d'un festin
     Fit que de ta route ordinaire,
     Tu reculas vers le matin:
     Et d'un esmerveillable change   65
     Te couchas aux rives du Gange:

D'où vient que ta severité
Moindre qu'en la faute d'Atree
Ne punit point ceste contree,
D'une eternelle obscurité? 70

VIII Non, non, tu luis sur le coulpable,
Comme tu fais sur l'innocent:
Ta Nature n'est point capable
Du trouble qu'une Ame ressent:
Tu dois ta flamme à tout le monde: 75
Et ton alleure vagabonde,
Comme une servile action
Qui dépend d'une autre puissance,
N'ayant aucune connoissance,
N'a point aussi d'affection. 80

IX Mais, ô planette belle et claire,
Je ne parle pas sagement:
Le juste excez de la colere
M'a faict perdre le jugement:
Ce traistre, quelque frenesie 85
Qui travaillast sa fantaisie,
Eut encor assez de raison,
Pour ne vouloir rien entreprendre,
Bel Astre, qu'il n'eust veu descendre
Ta lumiere sous l'Orizon. 90

X Au poinct qu'il écuma sa rage,
Le Dieu de Seine estoit dehors
A regarder croistre l'ouvrage
Dont ce Prince embellit ses bords:
Il se reserra tout à l'heure 95
Au plus bas lieu de sa demeure:
Et ses Nymphes dessous les eaux
Toutes sans voix, et sans haleine,
Pour se cacher furent en peine
De trouver assez de roseaux. 100

XI   La terreur des choses passees,
A leurs yeux se ramentevant,
Faisoit prevoir à leurs pensees
Plus de malheurs qu'auparavant:
Et leur estoit si peu croyable,   105
Qu'en cet accident effroyable
Personne les peust secourir,
Que pour en estre dégagees
Le Ciel les auroit obligees
S'il leur eust permis de mourir.   110

XII   Revenez belles fugitives:
Dequoy versez-vous tant de pleurs?
Asseurez vos Ames craintives:
Remettez vos chappeaux de fleurs:
Le Roy vit, et ce miserable,   115
Ce monstre vrayment déplorable,
Qui n'avoit jamais espreuvé
Que peut un visage d'Alcide,
A commencé le parricide,
Mais il ne l'a pas achevé.   120

XIII   Pucelles qu'on se resjouysse:
Mettez-vous l'esprit en repos:
Que ceste peur s'evanoüisse:
Vous la prenez mal à propos:
Le Roy vit et les destinees   125
Luy gardent un nombre d'annees,
Qui fera maudire le Sort
A ceux dont l'aveugle manie
Dresse des plants de tyrannie
Pour bastir quand il sera mort.   130

XIV   O bien-heureuse intelligence,
Puissance quiconque tu sois,
Dont la fatale diligence
Preside à l'Empire François:
Toutes ces visibles merveilles   135

De soins, de peines, et de veilles,
Qui jamais ne t'ont peu lasser,
N'ont-elles pas faict une Histoire
Qu'en la plus ingrate memoire
L'oubly ne sçauroit effacer? 140

XV Ces Archers aux casaques peintes
Ne peuvent pas n'estre surpris,
Ayans à combattre les feintes
De tant d'infidelles Esprits:
Leur presence n'est qu'une pompe: 145
Avecques peu d'art on les trompe:
Mais de quelle dexterité
Se peut déguiser une audace,
Qu'en l'Ame aussi-tost qu'en la face
Tu n'en lises la verité? 150

XVI Grand Demon d'eternelle marque,
Fais qu'il te souvienne tousjours
Que tous nos maux en ce Monarque
Ont leur refuge et leur secours:
Et qu'arrivant l'heure prescrite, 155
Que le trespas qui tout limite
Nous privera de sa valeur,
Nous n'avons jamais eu d'alarmes
Où nous ayons versé des larmes
Pour une semblable douleur. 160

XVII Je sçay bien que par la Justice,
Dont la paix accroist le pouvoir,
Il faict demeurer la malice
Aux bornes de quelque devoir:
Et que son invincible espee, 165
Sous telle influence est trempee,
Qu'elle met la frayeur par tout
Aussi-tost qu'on la voit reluire:
Mais quand le mal-heur nous veut nuire,
De quoy ne vient-il point à bout? 170

XVIII   Soit que l'ardeur de la priere
　　　　Le tienne devant un Autel,
　　　　Soit que l'honneur à la barriere
　　　　L'appelle à debattre un cartel:
　　　　Soit que dans la chambre il médite,   175
　　　　Soit qu'aux bois la chasse l'invite,
　　　　Jamais ne t'escarte si loin
　　　　Qu'aux embusches qu'on luy peut tendre
　　　　Tu ne sois prest à le deffendre,
　　　　Sitost qu'il en aura besoin.   180

XIX   Garde sa compagne fidelle,
　　　　Cette Reine dont les Bontez
　　　　De nostre foiblesse mortelle
　　　　Tous les defaux ont surmontez,
　　　　Fay que jamais rien ne l'enuye,   185
　　　　Que toute infortune la fuye:
　　　　Et qu'aux roses de sa Beauté
　　　　L'âge par qui tout se consume
　　　　Redonne contre sa coustume
　　　　La grace de la nouveauté.   190

XX   Serre d'une estrainte si ferme
　　　　Le nœud de leurs chastes amours,
　　　　Que la seule mort soit le terme
　　　　Qui puisse en arrester le cours:
　　　　Beny les plaisirs de leur couche,   195
　　　　Et fay renaistre de leur souche
　　　　Des scions si beaux, et si vers,
　　　　Que de leur fueillage sans nombre,
　　　　A jamais ils puissent faire ombre
　　　　Aux peuples de tout l'Univers.   200

XXI   Sur tout pour leur commune joye,
　　　　Devide aux ans de leur Daufin,
　　　　A longs filets d'or, et de soye,
　　　　Un bon-heur qui n'ait point de fin:
　　　　Quelques vœux que face l'envie,   205
　　　　Conserve-leur sa chere vie:

>   Et tiens par elle ensevelis
>   D'une bonace continuë
>   Les Aquilons dont sa venuë
>   A guaranty les fleurs de Lys.   210
>
> XXII   Conduis-le sous leur asseurance
>   Promptement jusques au sommet
>   De l'indubitable esperance
>   Que son enfance leur promet:
>   Et pour achever leurs journees,   215
>   Que les Oracles ont bornees
>   Dedans le trosne imperial,
>   Avant que le Ciel les appelle,
>   Fais leur ouyr ceste nouvelle
>   Qu'il a razé l'Escurial. [2]   220

* * *

Professor Wadsworth's analysis and critique will establish the ode's main topics and its special problems of integration.

> Stanzas 1-6. Introduction. Barbarism of the age (1-2); praise for the greatest of kings (3-4); ingratitude of his troublemaking subjects (5-6). 7-9. Apostrophe to the Sun: why didn't you change your course and plunge the country into darkness [during the attempted assassination]? This idea rejected as irrational. 10-13. Horror of the God of the Seine and of his nymphs. The poet reassures them: the King has escaped injury. 14-22. Addressed to the "bienheureuse intelligence" which presides over France's destiny. Continue to watch over the King (14-18) and protect the Queen (19). Bless their union with many offspring (20). Take care of the *dauphin* and make him a great conquerer (21-22). [3]

Because three sections "seem unnecessary to the poem's development" — namely, the solar apostrophe, the incident of the river spirits, and the requests made to France's patroness on behalf of

---

[2] Malherbe, I, pp. 71-78.
[3] Wadsworth, p. 191.

the King's family — Professor Wadsworth concludes that the ode may "suffer from a certain discontinuity or lack of direction." [4] The poem's direction will become clear, I believe, upon disclosure of its interwoven patterns of analogy.

The Descent of Man

In the opening section, the poet describes the "siecle de nos Peres" (v. 13), when France was "Pleine de meurs, et de courages, / Qu'on ne pouvoit assez loüer" (vv. 16-17). By contrast, the French of the poet's own time stand condemned as "ingrats... / Barbares et desnaturez" (vv. 41-42). Finally, the speaker addresses his exordium to "races futures" (v. 1), who will apparently have recaptured some of the moral rectitude of the distant past: the poet doubts if they will read or hear of today's impieties "sans rougir de honte" (v. 5). This system of motifs — a moral decline from one generation to another, followed by the advent of a new race — recalls a familiar pattern of myth, the Ages of Man, wherein an age of bronze, bellicose but god-fearing, preceded an age of iron when, according to Ovid,

> All manner of crime broke out; modesty, truth and loyalty fled. Treachery and trickery took their place, deceit and violence and criminal greed.... All proper affection lay vanquished and, last of the immortals, Justice left the blood-soaked earth. [5]

To punish the offenders, Zeus flooded the world, after which he created "a new stock of men, unlike the former ones, a race of miraculous origin." [6] This oblique and half-buried analogy between the Ages of Man and the generations of the French serves to evoke the possibility of a social or political disaster comparable to the Flood in its potential for devastation. To prevent such a catastrophe, the nation's patroness must intervene. But how? In

---

[4] Wadsworth, p. 192.
[5] *The Metamorphoses*, transl. Mary Innes (Baltimore: Penguin Books, 1955), pp. 32-33.
[6] Ovid, p. 36.

the following exhortation to that mysterious force, there may be a clue; the apparent subject is the Queen:

> Et qu'aux roses de sa Beauté
> L'âge par qui tout se consume
> Redonne contre sa coustume
> La grace de la nouveauté.   (vv. 187-190)

As Professor Wadsworth pointed out, the section from which this wish is extracted seems logically unconnected to the rest of the ode. But granting the metonymic relationship between sovereign and subjects, a figurative reading may be proposed with implications for the motif of man's descent. Both this passage and the motif in question share the idea of decadence through time — physical, in the case of the Queen; moral, in the case of her subjects. If, however, the patroness of France granted the poet's wish and reversed the effects of passing time, then she would not only renew the Queen's beauty, but above all, she would assure purification of the French conscience. From this it follows that the "races futures" would be the natural progeny, not the specially created successors of the "race actuelle."

Revolt

The poet presents Henri IV as at least semidivine:

> Et qui peut nier qu'apres Dieu,
> Sa gloire qui n'a point d'exemples,
> N'ait merité que dans nos temples
> On luy donne le second lieu?   (vv. 27-30)

Far from being universally revered, however, the King has many antagonists in the "race actuelle." The populace is troublesome, "d'un courage forcené, / Rejettant son obeïssance" (vv. 47-48); Jean Châtel, an earlier assailant, ranks as an "esprit farouche, / ... sorty des ombres d'Enfer" (vv. 51-52); and Jacques des Isles, who attempted to unhorse the King is "un autre perfide, / Où la mesme audace reside" (vv. 55-56). Moreover, the King's allies and retainers are a particularly helpless lot: seeing Jacques des Isles attack the King, the Seine god "se reserra tout à l'heure / Au plus bas lieu de sa demeure" (vv. 95-96); meanwhile, his nymphs "pour se cacher furent en peine / De trouver assez de roseaux" (vv. 99-100); the archers assigned to protect the King lack the perceptiveness necessary to their task, for "avecques peu d'art on les trompe" (v. 146); and finally, the poet himself, rendered irrational by events, suffers from a "juste exces de la colere" (v. 83). The solar apostrophe functions as a gauge of this "exces," for in it the poet not only scolds the sun for failing to plunge France into darkness at the moment of the madman's assault on the King, but above all, he bases his reproach upon what appears to be a thoroughly confused version of the Atreus myth. According to the poet, the sun had previously darkened the world out of "horreur d'un festin" (v. 62), that is, the one at which Atreus served to his brother Thyestes a stew composed of the limbs of Thyestes' own sons. In all common versions of the myth, however, the sun reversed its course by order of Zeus during a different episode of the fraternal rivalry: when Thyestes debauched the wife of Atreus and usurped the latter's throne. There is a little-known variant, found only in Seneca's play *Thyestes,* which parallels Malherbe's version. His use of the unfamiliar variant serves to create the impression of intellectual disorder in a man under great pressure.

The King's sole protector is the patroness to whom Malherbe addresses the final stanzas of the ode. That Henri IV survived the various attempts made upon his life is nothing less than "visibles merveilles / De soins, de peines, et de veilles, / Qui jamais ne t'ont peu lasser" (vv. 135-137). To destroy the enemies of France, the poet asks that the "bienheureuse intelligence" nurture a new hero. None other than the *dauphin,* to whose fortunes the final stanzas are devoted, this warrior will, with the patroness's aid, raze the Escorial (v. 220).

The complex of motifs just described is both elaborate and well integrated: a superhuman king attacked by one or two agents of the underworld; his followers thrown into disarray; his sole protection residing in a vague power of destiny which may one day furnish a hero capable of defeating his enemies. Again, the motifs evoke a specific pattern of myth, that of the Giants' revolt against Zeus. The rebels, having escaped from Tartarus, sought to overthrow the divine order by scaling Olympus and attacking the gods, some of whom — Hestia and Demeter in particular — were seized not only with indignation, but above all with panic. Fate, however, chose to save Olympus, and after protecting it for some time, sent Hercules to cast the Giants back down into darkness. Thus the current French crisis is seen in cosmic terms, which show how greatly the world order depends on the security of the French throne, and how greatly that security depends on the operation of the most inscrutable forces.

But if this pair of allusions places in cosmic perspective the poet's pessimistic beliefs about the French condition in his own time, they scarcely assure the poem's total coherence. Converging only upon certain relations among the antagonists, they do not present with sufficient exhaustiveness or rigor the adversaries' particular powers or dispositions. To solve all of these problems, Malherbe significantly extended his poetic technique by embedding in both allusions the same system of complementary stylistic features.

Chiaroscuro

Pervading the ode is a kind of Manichean struggle where darkness and light (the latter in a spectrum ranging from yellow to pink) appear as physical attributes and as symbols of moral or intellectual qualities. The forces of light include such superhuman personages as Zeus, whose sign of anger, the thunderbolt, appears as "tonnerre" (v. 8); the Sun, that "grand luminaire" (v. 61), the nymphs of the Seine and the "bienheureuse intelligence." The last two are associated with light because of their perspicacity or *clartés*. The nymphs, who witnessed Jacques des Isles' assassination attempt, grasped the meaning of events:

> La terreur des choses passees,
> A leurs yeux se ramentevant,
> Faisoit prevoir à leurs pensees
> Plus de malheurs qu'auparavant.   (vv. 101-104)

For her part, the patroness can see through the ruses of traitors:

> Mais de quelle dexterité
> Se peut déguiser une audace,
> Qu'en l'Ame aussi-tost qu'en la face
> Tu n'en lises la verité?   (vv. 147-150)

The humans associated with light include the "races futures" who will not read of today's impieties "sans rougir de honte" (v. 5), and the royal family. The King's "gloire" (v. 28) and his "tige Illustre" (v. 36) both contain the idea of a burst of light (from Latin *gloria* and *illustris*), as does the epithet "Alcide" (v. 118), Hercules' patronymic which means "glory of Hera"; finally one sees his attribute, a sword, "reluire" (v. 168). The Queen's chief feature, her physical beauty, appears as "roses" (v. 187), conventionally pink. As for the *dauphin,* the poet wishes that the young man's life be measured out in brilliant "filets d'or" (v. 203). The forces of darkness include all of the King's antagonists: the "race actuelle" is, in general, blacker than black, for by its actions France "s'est faict aujourd'huy si tragique, / Qu'elle produit ce que l'Affrique / Auroit vergongne d'avoüer" (vv. 18-20); Jean Châtel, as mentioned before, emerged from the "ombres d'Enfer" (v. 52); and the act of Jacques des Isles requires punishment in kind for the whole country, "une eternelle obscurité" (v. 70). Finally, Malherbe links Spain to darkness by the synechdochal reference to the Escorial (v. 220). It is crucial to the poem's structure that this edifice commemorates Philip II's defeat of France in 1557 at Saint-Quentin, and that its name derives from the Latin *scoria,* a term meaning dross or slag, both being dark substances.

Until the final stanza darkness enjoys a major advantage over light: a high degree of purposive mobility. As subjects and members of the present race, the poet indicates, "tousjours nous assaillons sa teste / De quelque nouvelle tempeste" (vv. 45-46). Jean Châtel, confronted the King and "d'un coup sanglant frappa sa bouche" (v. 53). The King, however, is usually represented as motionless: in the wish that "dans nos temples / On luy donne le second lieu" (vv. 29-30), he resembles a statue, just as he does later, when "l'ardeur de la priere / Le tienne devant un Autel" (vv. 171-172). His marriage has a paradoxical air of immobility, even bondage, being "une estrainte si ferme" (v. 191). It is this condition that renders the King utterly dependent on the protection given by the "bienheureuse intelligence."

The final stanza, however, contains an important change in the stylistic pattern. The poet hopes that the *dauphin* will live up to his great promise, and that the King and Queen (stationary on their thrones) will hear "avant que le Ciel les appelle, / ... qu'il a razé l'Escurial" (vv. 218 and 220). What the poet in fact desires is nothing less than the miraculous exchange of the antagonists' secondary properties. Light, in the person of the *dauphin*, will acquire the vigorous mobility that had made of darkness such a threat to light, and with this power he will reduce to nothingness the seat of triumphant darkness. If such a miracle occurred, the world order could indeed be saved and the world's age of greatness might indeed begin anew.

To sum up, Malherbe painted a coherent picture of France at the and of its powers: almost morally bankrupt, it surely nears collapse. With its great king curiously impotent and protected by a vague power of destiny, diabolical forces seek to topple him and succeed in spreading panic and rage among his allies and loyal subjects. In this *monde ébranlé*, only the most paradoxical solutions remain conceivable: a reversal of time to recapture the age of gold; or the advent of a messianic hero who, strengthened by forces sapped from the enemy, will cast the latter down. That all of these solutions exist in a hypothetical future serves only to reinforce the impression of anguish with which the poet viewed his world. [7]

---

[7] For the persistence of these themes in the work of Corneille, see Louisa A. Jones, "The Position of the King in *Le Cid*," *F. R.* 40 (1967), 643-646.

IV

THE POETICS OF GRANDEUR

In April, 1606, while at work on his second major ode, Malherbe began writing the third. Professor Fromilhague has summarized as follows the historical background of the new poem:

> Henri de la Tour d'Auvergne, vicomte de Turenne, maréchal de Bouillon, s'était révolté contre Henri IV et fortifié dans Sedan, dont il était prince. Pour le réduire à l'obéissance, le roi quitte Paris le 15 mars 1606 à la tête de ses troupes. Mais à peine a-t-il paru devant la place que Bouillon se soumet (2 avril).[1]

* * *

AU FEU ROY

SUR L'HEUREUX SUCCEZ DU

VOYAGE DE SEDAN

I   Enfin apres les tempestes
Nous voicy rendus au port:
Enfin nous voyons nos testes
Hors de l'injure du Sort.
Nous n'avons rien qui menace   5

---

[1] Malherbe, II, p. 17.

De troubler nostre bonace:
Et ces matieres de pleurs,
Massacres, feux, et rapines,
De leurs funestes espines
Ne gasteront plus nos fleurs.   10

II Nos prieres sont ouyes,
Tout est reconcilié:
Nos peurs sont esvanoüyes,
Sedan s'est humilié.
A peine il a veu le foudre   15
Party pour le mettre en poudre
Que faisant comparaison
De l'espoir, et de la crainte,
Pour éviter la contrainte
Il s'est mis à la raison.   20

III Qui n'eust creu que ses murailles,
Que deffendoit un Lyon,
N'eussent faict des funerailles
Plus que n'en fit Ilion:
Et qu'avant qu'estre à la feste   25
De si penible conqueste,
Les champs se fussent vestus
Deux fois de robbe nouvelle,
Et le fer eust en javelle
Deux fois les bleds abbatus?   30

IV Et toutesfois, ô merveille!
Mon Roy, l'exemple des Roys,
Dont la grandeur nompareille
Fait qu'on adore ses Loix,
Accompagné d'un genie   35
Qui les volontez manie,
L'a sçeu tellement presser
D'obeyr et de se rendre,
Qu'il n'a pas eu pour le prendre
Loisir de le menacer.   40

V Tel qu'à vagues espanduës
Marche un fleuve imperieux,
De qui les neiges fonduës
Rendent le cours furieux,
Rien n'est seur en son rivage: 45
Ce qu'il treuve il le ravage:
Et traisnant comme buissons,
Les chesnes, et leurs racines,
Oste aux campagnes voisines
L'esperance des moissons. 50

VI Tel, et plus espouvantable,
S'en alloit ce conquerant,
A son pouvoir indomptable
Sa colere mesurant:
Son front avoit une audace 55
Telle que Mars en la Thrace:
Et les esclairs de ses yeux
Estoient comme d'un tonnerre,
Qui gronde contre la terre,
Quand elle a fasché les Cieux. 60

VII Quelle vaine resistence
A son puissant appareil,
N'eust porté la penitence
Qui suit un mauvais conseil!
Et veu sa faute bornee 65
D'une cheute infortunee,
Comme la rebellion,
Dont la fameuse folie
Fit voir à la Thessalie
Olympe sur Pelion? 70

VIII Voyez comme en son courage,
Quand on se renge au devoir,
La pitié calme l'orage
Que l'ire a faict esmouvoir:
A peine fut reclamee, 75

    Sa douceur accoustumee,
    Que d'un sentiment humain,
    Frappé non moins que de charmes,
    Il fit la paix, et les armes
    Luy tomberent de la main.   80

IX Arriere vaines chimeres
    De haines, et de rancueurs:
    Soupçons de choses ameres
    Esloignez-vous de nos cœurs:
    Loin, bien loin, tristes pensees,   85
    Où nos miseres passees
    Nous avoient ensevelis:
    Sous HENRY c'est ne voir goutte,
    Que de revoquer en doute
    Le salut des Fleurs de Lis.   90

X O Roy, qui du rang des hommes,
    T'exceptes par ta Bonté,
    Roy qui de l'âge où nous sommes
    Tout le mal as surmonté:
    Si tes labeurs, d'où la France   95
    A tiré sa delivrance,
    Sont escrits avecques foy,
    Qui sera si ridicule
    Qui ne confesse qu'Hercule
    Fut moins Hercule que toy?   100

XI De combien de tragedies,
    Sans ton asseuré secours,
    Estoient les trames ourdies
    Pour ensanglanter nos jours?
    Et qu'auroit faict l'innocence,   105
    Si l'outrageuse licence,
    De qui le souverain bien
    Est d'opprimer, et de nuire,
    N'eust treuvé pour la destruire
    Un bras fort comme le tien?   110

XII Mon Roy, cognois ta puissance,
Elle est capable de tout,
Tes desseins n'ont pas naissance
Qu'on en voit deja le bout:
Et la fortune amoureuse   115
De ta vertu genereuse,
Treuve de si doux appas
A te servir, et te plaire,
Que c'est la mettre en cholere
Que de ne l'employer pas.   120

XIII Use de sa bien-vueillance,
Et luy donne ce plaisir,
Qu'elle suive ta vaillance
A quelque nouveau desir:
Où que tes bannieres aillent,   125
Quoy que tes armes assaillent,
Il n'est orgueil endurcy,
Que brisé comme du verre,
A tes pieds elle n'attere,
S'il n'implore ta mercy.   130

XIV Je sçay bien que les Oracles
Predisent tous qu'à ton fils
Sont reservez les miracles
De la prise de Menfis:
Et que c'est luy dont l'espee   135
Au sang barbare trempee,
Quelque jour apparoissant,
A la Grece qui souspire,
Fera décroistre l'Empire
De l'infidelle Croissant.   140

XV Mais tandis que les annees
Pas à pas font avancer,
L'âge où de ses destinees
La gloire doit commencer:
Que fais-tu que d'une armee   145
A te venger animee,

Tu ne mets dans le tombeau
Ces voisins, dont les pratiques
De nos rages domestiques
Ont allumé le flambeau? 150

XVI Quoy que les Alpes chenuës
Les couvrent de toutes parts,
Et facent monter aux nuës
Leurs effroyables ramparts:
Alors que de ton passage 155
On leur fera le message,
Qui verront-elles venir,
Envoyé sous tes auspices,
Qu'aussi-tost leurs precipices
Ne se laissent applanir? 160

XVII Croy moy, contente l'envie
Qu'ont tant de jeunes guerriers,
D'aller exposer leur vie
Pour t'aquerir des Lauriers:
Et ne tiens point ocieuses 165
Ces Ames ambitieuses,
Qui jusques où le matin
Met les Estoilles en fuitte,
Oseront sous ta conduite
Aller querir du butin. 170

XVIII Desja le Tezin tout morne,
Consulte de se cacher,
Voulant guarantir sa corne
Que tu luy dois arracher:
Et le Pò, tombe certaine 175
De l'audace trop hautaine,
Tenant baissé le menton,
Dans sa caverne profonde,
S'appreste à voir en son Onde
Choir un autre Phaëton. 180

XIX   Va, Monarque Magnanime,
Souffre à ta juste douleur,
Qu'en leurs rives elle imprime
Les marques de ta valeur:
L'Astre, dont la course ronde   185
Tous les jours voit tout le Monde,
N'aura point achevé l'an,
Que tes conquestes ne razent
Tout le Piémont, et n'écrazent
La couleuvre de Milan.   190

XX   Ce sera là que ma lire,
Faisant son dernier effort,
Entreprendra de mieux dire
Qu'un Cyne prés de sa mort:
Et se rendant favorable   195
Ton oreille incomparable
Te forcera d'avoüer,
Qu'en l'aise de la victoire,
Rien n'est si doux que la gloire
De se voir si bien loüer.   200

XXI   Il ne faut pas que tu penses
Treuver de l'eternité,
En ces pompeuses despenses
Qu'invente la vanité:
Tous ces chefs-d'œuvres antiques   205
Ont à peine leurs reliques:
Par les Muses seulement
L'homme est exempt de la Parque:
Et ce qui porte leur marque
Demeure eternellement.   210

XXII   Par elles traçant l'histoire
De tes faicts laborieux,
Je deffendray ta memoire
Du trespas injurieux,
Et quelque assaut que te face   215
L'oubly par qui tout s'efface,

> Ta loüange dans mes vers
> D'Amaranthe couronnee
> N'aura sa fin terminee
> Qu'en celle de l'Univers. ²

> 220

* * *

Examining the text itself, Professor Wadsworth discovered in the order and articulation of its themes a "high degree of density and coherence":

> Stanzas 1-4. Expression of relief that peace is restored, and sooner than expected. Transition (4) to the prowess of the King. 5-7. The wrath of the King and his army, marching off to war. 8-9. The King's mildness, upon receiving Sedan's surrender. 10-13. Praise for Henri IV and his accomplishments. 14-19. Exhortation to the King: while waiting for his son to become a great military hero he should himself stamp out France's enemies — Savoy, Piedmont, etc. 20-22. The power of poetry: the Muses will help me make your name immortal. ³

Even if the third ode more nearly approximates logical unity than either studied so far, there nevertheless remain two sections which appear unnecessary. "The allusion to the *dauphin*," states Professor Wadsworth, "may seem out of place, but it is really rather brief and parenthetical." ⁴ Secondly, the conclusion is problematic. Here Professor Wadsworth and Professor Fromilhague agree, at least in part. Professor Fromilhague notes that the nineteenth stanza posesses all of the epic features contained in the finales of the first and second odes. ⁵ But while Professor Fromilhague proceeds from this observation to the judgment that stanzas 20-22 may therefore be suppressed without harming the poem's construction, ⁶ Professor Wadsworth concludes that the final stanzas are at least related to the poem's chief idea:

---

² Malherbe, I, pp. 63-70.
³ Wadsworth, p. 192.
⁴ *Ibid.*
⁵ *La Vie de Malherbe: apprentissage et luttes* (Paris: Colin, 1954), pp. 196-198. Also cited by Professor Wadsworth, p. 192.
⁶ Fromilhague, *op. cit.*, p. 197.

The finale, dealing with Malherbe's powers as a poet, is perhaps an after-thought inspired by his own deep satisfaction with this particular work. But this theme, like all the others, is skillfully linked to the core of the poem. Everywhere, from beginning to end, the greatness of Henri IV is being demonstrated: as peacemaker, as warmaker, at Sedan, in the past, in the future, in the annals of history.[7]

An inspection of allusion and style in this ode indeed corroborates Professor Wadsworth's belief: the King's greatness *is* the key to the poem's structure and meaning. Still, this greatness, while implicating his military and political acts, is more deeply enmeshed in the King's transcendence of human limits.

The Image of Hercules

Two details of the narrative are particularly striking. First, the King has pacified and united France after a long embroilment in civil and religious disorder, of which the Bouillon episode was the final incident:

> Enfin apres les tempestes
> Nous voicy rendus au port:
> Enfin nous voyons nos testes
> Hors de l'injure du Sort.
> Nous n'avons rien qui menace
> De troubler nostre bonace. (vv. 1-6)

Secondly, as father of his country, Henri has surpassed an ancient hero to whom the poet has previously compared him:

> Si tes labeurs, d'où la France
> A tiré sa delivrance,
> Sont escrits avecques foy,
> Qui sera si ridicule
> Qui ne confesse qu'Hercule
> Fut moins Hercule que toy? (vv. 95-100)

---

[7] Wadsworth, p. 192.

This conjunction is arresting. Indeed, it suggests a partial identification — not of Henri IV and Hercules — but rather of Henri IV and a third hero whose life not only parallels that of the French king but who, above all, admired and emulated Hercules. This hero is none other than Theseus of Athens. The general outline of Theseus's career (as related by Plutarch) and that of Malherbe's Henri IV are in fact virtually indistinguishable.

The careers of Theseus and Henri IV share three motifs. The first, already discussed, has reference to the hero's political consolidation of the turbulent area over which he reigns. (Incidental to this motif is the fact that neither Theseus nor Henri IV acceded to his rightful kingship without defeating fierce opposition: in Greece, Pallas and his fifty sons; in France the Catholic League and — after the wars of religion — dissident Protestants like Bouillon.) Once having secured the throne and the nation, each hero felt the lure of foreign adventure. This temptation constitutes the second motif. It is in the character of the temptation, the hero's response, and the political consequences of the response that appear the first important differences of detail between the legend of Theseus and the life of the King. For Theseus, the adventures were as often sexual as military; in any event, they contributed nothing to the national good, and at times they even jeopardized it. These escapades — Anaxo's abduction, the war of the Lapiths against the Centaurs, the war with the Amazons, and the ill-fated journey with Pirithous, his companion in lechery, during which they abducted Helen and suffered imprisonment in Hades for attempting to abduct Proserpine — show Theseus arrogantly following his violent and lustful penchants instead of satisfying his royal obligations. Consequently Theseus became estranged from the Athenians. On his return from Hades, he found himself not only hated and scorned by the populace, but outmanoeuvred by hostile political factions. Unable to regain power, he went into exile. Like Theseus, Henri IV must consider the possibility of foreign adventure, but his adversaries differ radically from the Amazons or Centaurs:

> Ces voisins, dont les pratiques
> De nos rages domestiques
> Ont allumé le flambeau.   (vv. 148-150)

Genuine threats to the internal and external security of France, Savoy and the Piedmont are fit objects of the aggression that the speaker urges upon his King. The speaker's argumentation points to another feature which distinguishes Henri IV from Theseus:

> Mon Roy, cognois ta puissance,
> Elle est capable de tout,
> Tes desseins n'ont pas naissance
> Qu'on en voit deja le bout:
> Et la fortune amoureuse
> De ta vertu genereuse,
> Treuve de si doux appas
> A te servir, et te plaire,
> Que c'est la mettre en cholere
> Que de ne l'employer pas.   (vv. 111-120)

If Theseus erred tragically by acting, the peace-loving Henri IV risks fortune's reprisal by *failing* to act. Moreover, Henri IV, in his foreign military adventures, will, unlike Theseus, enjoy the support of his subjects. The latter include not only the loyalists but also the ambitious and greedy who, in the absence of a war promising pillage, might organize the kind of anti-royal movement that greeted Theseus on his return from Hades:

> Croy moy, contente l'envie
> Qu'ont tant de jeunes guerriers,
> D'aller exposer leur vie
> Pour t'aquerir des Lauriers:
> Et ne tiens point ocieuses
> Ces Ames ambitieuses,
> Qui jusques où le matin
> Met les Estoilles en fuitte,
> Oseront sous ta conduite
> Aller querir du butin.   (vv. 161-170)

Thus, in his foreign adventures, the King is destined to succeed precisely where Theseus failed.

Besides nation-founding and foreign adventure, the careers of Theseus and Henri IV share a third motif, which concerns posterity. Continuation of the self has two aspects: first, reputation; secondly, blood succession. The legend of Theseus contains a set of circumstances which, while not disgraceful, lacks luster. The

Greek hero's murder — at the hand of Lycomedes of Scyros — went practically unnoticed in Athens where the usurper Menestheus had replaced Theseus on the throne. Even when Theseus's sons Acamas and Demoöphon returned from their military service at Troy and regained control of Attica, their father's memory was little respected. Only after his ghost appeared at Marathon and led a charge of Greeks against the Medes did Theseus receive a tomb and the sacrifices due a demi-god. Nor did his sons distinguish themselves as continuators of their father's earlier political policies; like him, they pursued other adventures, spectacular but ultimately worthless to Attica. In Malherbe's view Henri IV will enjoy a more felicitious posterity than Theseus. In the final stanzas of this ode — those which logical analysis is forced to find superfluous — the speaker explains that Henri's fame is already being assured:

> Ce sera là que ma lire,
> Faisant son dernier effort,
> Entreprendra de mieux dire
> Qu'un Cyne prés de sa mort:
> Et se rendant favorable
> Ton oreille incomparable
> Te forcera d'avoüer,
> Qu'en l'aise de la victoire,
> Rien n'est si doux que la gloire
> De se voir si bien loüer.   (vv. 191-200)

The sturdiest monuments (even Theseus's tomb) must perish; hence to provide uninterrupted celebrity for the King's name and labors, the poet is indispensable:

> Il ne faut pas que tu penses
> Treuver de l'eternité,
> En ces pompeuses despenses
> Qu'invente la vanité:
> Tous ces chefs-d'œuvres antiques
> Ont à peine leurs reliques:
> Par les Muses seulement
> L'homme est exempt de la Parque:
> Et ce qui porte leur marque
> Demeure eternellement.   (vv. 201-210)

Therefore, the speaker concludes:

> Ta loüange dans mes vers
> D'Amaranthe couronnee
> N'aura sa fin terminee
> Qu'en celle de l'Univers. (vv. 217-220)

But without the posthumous fulfillment of Henri IV's policies, in all their ramifications, such everlasting praise would serve only as a bitter reminder of incomplete achievements and of promises unkept. The reference to the *dauphin* — whose logical role in the poem may be questionable — is thus indispensable to the inversion of the posterity motif. In contrast with Acamas and Demoöphon, the *dauphin* will bring his father's work to completion by launching a successful crusade against those powers which threaten the larger region of which France is the chief domain, i.e. Western Europe and Christendom:

> Je sçay bien que les Oracles
> Predisent tous qu'à ton fils
> Sont reservez les miracles
> De la prise de Menfis:
> Et que c'est luy dont l'espee
> Au sang barbare trempee,
> Quelque jour apparoissant,
> A la Grece qui souspire,
> Fera décroistre l'Empire
> De l'infidelle Croissant. (vv. 131-140)

Here as in the first completed ode, the King's greatness consists of perfecting in history a flawed mythological pattern. The full meaning of Henry IV's greatness, however, is embedded in the text's elaborate style.

ELEVATION AND LIGHT

Perfecting a pattern of myth requires moral superiority and even inner illumination; its reward is eminence and glory. It is not by accident that the terms denoting the prerequisites and the recompense contain the ideas of height and light: these very images pervade the third completed ode. Immediately recognized by their physical manifestations, the King's spiritual superiority and illumination are a moral equivalent to the power of Zeus:

> Et les esclairs de ses yeux
> Estoient comme d'un tonnerre,
> Qui gronde contre la terre,
> Quand elle a fasché les Cieux.   (vv. 57-60)

These traits are far from static. First, they permit the King to transcend the humanity of his contemporaries:

> O Roy, qui du rang des hommes,
> T'exceptes par ta Bonté,
> Roy qui de l'âge où nous sommes
> Tout le mal a *surmonté*.   (vv. 91-94; italics mine)

But if his virtue did not manifest itself in heroic action, the King would be little more than a contemplative and self-regulating figure, not unlike the conventional idea of a philosopher or monk. Hence the King engages in dangerous undertakings and in so doing draws even closer than Hercules himself to the deity glimpsed in his brilliant eyes (see *supra*). Those who are but ordinarily virtuous, and thus rank below the King on the moral scale, not only acknowledge his superiority, but, desirous themselves of perfection, they obey his commands. The speaker, for example, declares:

> Mon Roy, l'exemple des Roys,
> Dont la *grandeur* nompareille
> Fait qu'on adore ses Loix.   (vv. 32-34; italics mine)

This submission, in the etymological sense of that word, is coupled with supreme confidence in the nation's security:

> *Sous* HENRY c'est ne voir goutte,
> Que de revoquer en doute
> Le salut des Fleurs de Lis.   (vv. 88-90; italics mine)

Not all, however, acknowledge the towering and resplendent virtues of the King. Those who oppose Henri IV may engage in "resistence" (v. 61), used in its etymological sense of refusal to descend, as in deference. They may arrogantly raise "effroyables ramparts" (v. 154), to defend themselves against the force of the King's authority. They, too, desire the power proper to elevation; but with it, they would seek "le souverain bien ... d'opprimer" (vv. 107-108); they wish to press others down into subservience. Against these miscreants the King must take police action. If prudent, these opponents will respond as did Bouillon, whose fortress at Sedan "s'est humilié" (v. 14) without struggle. Others, not willing to go down cravenly, will fight, and on this account the speaker reminds the King as follows:

> Où que tes bannieres aillent,
> Quoy que tes armes assaillent,
> Il n'est orgueil endurcy,
> Que brisé comme du verre,
> *A tes pieds elle n'attere,*
> S'il n'implore ta mercy.   (vv. 125-130;
> italics mine)

Those who insist on fighting to the very end will not only lose, but will be twice lowered: first to the ground and secondly "dans le tombeau" (v. 147). Moreover, their regions will be leveled and their symbols — already base and vile — will be flattened:

> L'Astre, dont la course ronde
> Tous les jours voit tout le Monde,
> N'aura point achevé l'an,
> Que tes conquestes ne *razent*
> Tout le Piémont, et n'*écrazent*
> La couleuvre de Milan.   (vv. 185-190;
> italics mine)

Finally, the *dauphin*, as hereditary continuator of the King's policies, is represented as diminishing the haughty symbol of Islam, and the Ottoman Empire that would impose that symbol on Christian Europe ("ton fils / ... Fera décroistre l'Empire / De l'infidelle Croissant" [vv. 132, 139-140]).

Thus in the domain of time and space, the King's inner grandeur permits him to attain the highest level of moral perfection and secular authority. In the former case, elevation is direct for he raises himself; in the latter, elevation is indirect for he rises by the voluntary or forced descent of others. Moreover, now that the King has reached the age when "la gloire doit commencer" (v. 144), he will enjoy the fitting reward of inner illumination. (*Gloire,* as noted in the preceding chapter, contains the idea of a burst of light.) Indeed, he will bask not only in his own radiance, but also in its reflection cast by the eyes of an admiring world.

While the preceding paragraphs account for the underlying causes and essential nature of the King's excellence, they do not fully justify the poet's earlier statement that "Hercule / Fut moins Hercule que toy" (vv. 99-100). (The King's superiority to Hercules would of course imply his superiority to Theseus.) How can the King at the end of his labors more adequately exemplify the salient qualities of Hercules at the end of *his* career? It is particularly germane that Hercules never died, but was translated to Olympus and made factotum of the gods. He thus transcended the very human limits that, until the ode's crucial finale, Henri IV seems unable to escape. Indeed, were the poem to end at stanza 19, the original comparison with Hercules would seem ironic, even belittling. In the final stanzas Malherbe describes the future state of the King's career. Created by the poet, this condition, Malherbe strongly implies, is preferable to any sort of godhead:

> Il ne faut pas que tu penses
> Treuver de l'eternité,
> En ces pompeuses despenses
> Qu'invente la vanité:
> Tous ces chefs-d'œuvres antiques
> Ont à peine leurs reliques:
> Par les Muses seulement
> L'homme est exempt de la Parque:
> Et ce qui porte leur marque
> Demeure eternellement.
>
> Par elles traçant l'histoire
> De tes faicts laborieux,
> Je deffendray ta memoire
> Du trespas injurieux,
> Et quelque assaut que te face
> L'oubly par qui tout s'efface,
> Ta loüange dans mes vers
> D'Amaranthe couronnee
> N'aura sa fin terminee
> Qu'en celle de l'Univers.   (vv. 201-220)

First, the poetic image of Henri's deeds, like the body and personality of Hercules, will transcend time, as well as the necessity for commemoration in space. Unlike the very flawed Hercules, however, Henri IV will assume absolute perfection in this immortality, as is suggested by the circular form of the Amaranthus crown. Such perfection entails deliverance from relativity, which Hercules, a mere demi-god, was never to know on Olympus. Further, it would deliver the King's image from that force to which even Zeus must defer: *la Parque*. Thus by his poetics of grandeur Malherbe enabled Henri IV to attain the resplendent eminence of an ideal type, a norm against which all other sovereigns would be measured. In the fullest sense he would be "l'exemple des Roys" (v. 32).

V

THE GEMINI

Malherbe addressed the fourth completed ode to his chief patron after 1605: Roger de Saint Lary et de Termes, seigneur de Bellegarde, offspring of the family which had distinguished itself during the sixteenth and early seventeenth centuries by heroism at Cérisoles and in the Alpine campaign. Begun in 1608, the first version of this ode was completed the same year. Three-hundred forty lines long and exceedingly repetitious, it appeared in 1609. A new version — shorter by ten stanzas and radically altered both in the order and in the detail of the twenty-six remaining — appeared in 1611.[1] This chapter will be concerned with the definitive version of the fourth ode.

* * *

A MONSEIGNEUR LE DUC DE BELLEGARDE, GRAND ESCUYER DE FRANCE

I   A la fin c'est trop de silence
En si beau sujet de parler:
Le merite qu'on veut celer
Souffre une injuste violence:

---

[1] Malherbe, II, p. 42.

Belle-garde unique support 5
Où mes vœux ont trouvé leur port,
Que tarde ma paresse ingrate,
Que desja ton bruit nompareil
Aux bords du Tage, et de l'Eufrate,
N'a veu l'un et l'autre Soleil? 10

II Les Muses hautaines et braves,
Tiennent le flatter odieux,
Et comme parentes des Dieux
Ne parlent jamais en esclaves:
Mais aussi ne sont-elles pas 15
De ces Beautez dont les appas
Ne sont que rigueur, et que glace:
Et de qui le cerveau leger,
Quelque service qu'on leur face,
Ne se peut jamais obliger. 20

III La vertu, qui de leur estude
Est le fruict le plus precieux,
Sur tous les actes vicieux
Leur fait hayr l'ingratitude:
Et les agreables chansons 25
Par qui leurs doctes nourrissons
Sçavent charmer les destinées,
Recompensent un bon accueil
De loüages que les années
Ne mettent point dans le cercueil. 30

IV Les tiennes par moy publiées,
Je le jure sur les Autels,
En la memoire des mortels
Ne seront jamais oubliées:
Et l'éternité que promet 35
La montagne au double sommet,
N'est que mensonge et que fumée:
Ou je rendray cet Univers
Amoureux de ta renommée
Autant que tu l'és de mes vers. 40

V   Comme en cueillant une guirlande,
L'homme est d'autant plus travaillé,
Que le parterre est émaillé
D'une diversité plus grande:
Tant de fleurs de tant de costez,   45
Faisant paroistre en leurs beautez
L'artifice de la Nature:
Qu'il tient suspendu son desir,
Et ne sçait en ceste peinture
Ny que laisser, ny que choisir.   50

VI   Ainsi quand pressé de la honte,
Dont me fait rougir mon devoir,
Je veux mon œuvre concevoir
Qui pour toy les âges surmonte:
Tu me tiens les sens enchantez   55
De tant de rares qualitez,
Où brille un excez de lumiere,
Que plus je m'arreste à penser,
Laquelle sera la premiere,
Moins je sçay par où commencer.   60

VII   Si nommer en son parentage
Une longue suitte d'ayeux,
Que la gloire a mis dans les Cieux,
Est reputé grand avantage:
De qui n'est-il point reconnu,   65
Que tousjours les tiens ont tenu
Les charges les plus honorables,
Dont le merite, et la raison,
Quand les Destins sont favorables,
Parent une Illustre maison?   70

VIII   Qui ne sçait de quelles tempestes
Leur fatale main autresfois,
Portant la foudre de nos Rois,
Des Alpes a battu les testes?
Qui n'a veu dessous leurs combas,   75
Le Pô mettre les cornes bas?

　　　　Et les peuples de ses deux rives,
　　　　Dans la frayeur ensevelis,
　　　　Laisser leurs despoüilles captives
　　　　A la mercy des Fleurs de Lis?　　　　　　　　80

IX　　Mais de chercher aux sepultures
　　　　Des tesmoignages de valeur,
　　　　C'est à ceux qui n'ont rien du leur
　　　　Estimable aux races futures:
　　　　Non pas à toy qui revestu,　　　　　　　　85
　　　　De tous les dons que la vertu
　　　　Peut recevoir de la Fortune,
　　　　Connois que c'est que du vray bien,
　　　　Et ne veux pas comme la Lune
　　　　Luire d'autre feu que du tien.　　　　　　　　90

X　　Quand le Monstre infame d'Envie,
　　　　A qui rien de l'autruy ne plaist,
　　　　Tout lasche et perfide qu'il est,
　　　　Jette les yeux dessus ta vie:
　　　　Et te voit emporter le pris　　　　　　　　95
　　　　Des grands Cœurs, et des beaux Espris,
　　　　Dont aujourd'huy la France est pleine,
　　　　Est-il pas contrainct d'avoüer,
　　　　Qu'il a luy-mesme de la peine
　　　　A s'empescher de te loüer?　　　　　　　　100

XI　　Soit que l'honneur de la carriere
　　　　T'appelle à monter à cheval,
　　　　Soit qu'il se presente un rival
　　　　Pour la lice, ou pour la barriere,
　　　　Soit que tu donnes ton loisir　　　　　　　　105
　　　　A prendre quelque autre plaisir
　　　　Esloigné des molles delices:
　　　　Qui ne sçait que toute la Court
　　　　A regarder tes exercises,
　　　　Comme à des Theatres accourt?　　　　　　　　110

XII   Quand tu passas en Italie,
Où tu fus querir pour mon Roy
Ce joyau d'honneur, et de foy,
Dont l'Arne à la Seine s'allie:
Thetis ne suivit-elle pas   115
Ta bonne grace, et tes appas,
Comme un object émerveillable:
Et jura qu'avecque Jason
Jamais Argonaute semblable
N'alla conquerir la toison?   120

XIII   Tu menois le blond Hymenée,
Qui devoit solemnellement,
De ce fatal accouplement
Celebrer l'heureuse journée:
Jamais il ne fut si paré: 125
Jamais en son habit doré
Tant de richesses n'éclatterent:
Toutesfois les Nymphes du lieu,
Non sans apparence douterent
Qui de vous deux estoit le Dieu.   130

XIV   De combien de pareilles marques,
Dont on ne me peut démentir,
Ay-je dequoy te guarantir
Contre les menaces des Parques?
Si ce n'est qu'un si long discours   135
A de trop penibles détours:
Et qu'à bien dispenser les choses,
Il faut mesler pour un guerrier
A peu de Myrthe et peu de Roses,
Force Palme et force Laurier?   140

XV   Achille estoit haut de corsage:
L'or éclattoit en ses cheveux:
Et les Dames avecques veux
Souspiroient apres son visage:
Sa gloire à danser et chanter,   145
Tirer de l'arc, sauter, lutter,

A nulle autre n'estoit seconde:
Mais s'il n'eust rien eu de plus beau,
Son nom qui vole par le monde
Seroit-il pas dans le tombeau? 150

XVI S'il n'eust par un bras homicide,
Dont rien ne repoussoit l'effort,
Sur Ilion vengé le tort
Qu'avoit receu le jeune Atride:
De quelque adresse qu'au giron 155
Ou de Phenix, ou de Chiron,
Il eust faict son apprentissage,
Nostre âge auroit-il aujourd'huy
Le memorable tesmoignage
Que la Grece a donné de luy? 160

XVII C'est aux magnanimes exemples,
Qui sous la banniere de Mars
Sont faits au milieu des hazards,
Qu'il appartient d'avoir des Temples:
Et c'est avecques ces couleurs, 165
Que l'histoire de nos malheurs
Marquera si bien ta memoire,
Que tous les siecles avenir
N'auront point de nuict assez noire,
Pour en cacher le souvenir. 170

XVIII En ce long-temps, où les manies
D'un nombre infiny de mutins,
Poussez de nos mauvais destins,
Ont assouvy leurs felonnies,
Par quels faits d'armes valeureux, 175
Plus que nul autre aventureux,
N'as-tu mis ta gloire en estime?
Et declaré ta passion,
Contre l'espoir illegitime
De la rebelle ambition? 180

XIX Tel que d'un effort difficile
Un fleuve au travers de la Mer,
Sans que son goust devienne amer,
Passe d'Elide en la Sicile:
Ses flots par moyens inconnus   185
En leur douceur entretenus
Aucun meslange ne reçoivent:
Et dans Syracuse arrivant
Sont treuvez de ceux qui les boivent
Aussi peu salez que devant.   190

XX Tel entre ces Esprits tragiques,
Ou plustost demons insensez,
Qui de nos dommages passez
Tramoient les funestes pratiques,
Tu ne t'és jamais diverty,   195
De suivre le juste party:
Mais blasmant l'impure licence
De leurs desloyales humeurs,
As tousjours aymé l'innocence,
Et pris plaisir aux bonnes meurs.   200

XXI Depuis que pour sauver sa terre,
Mon Roy, le plus grand des humains,
Eut laissé partir de ses mains
Le premier trait de son tonnerre,
Jusqu'à la fin de ses exploits,   205
Que tout eut reconnu ses lois,
A t'il jamais défait armée,
Pris ville, ny forcé rampart,
Où ta valeur accoustumée
N'ait eu la principale part?   210

XXII Soit que pres de Seine et de Loire
Il pavast les plaines de morts:
Soit que le Rosne outre ses bords
Luy vist faire éclatter sa gloire:
Ne l'as-tu pas tousjours suivy?   215
Ne l'as-tu pas tousjours servy?

Et tousjours par dignes ouvrages
Tesmoigné le mespris du Sort
Que sçait imprimer aux courages
Le soin de vivre apres la mort?   220

XXIII Mais quoy? ma barque vagabonde
Est dans les Syrtes bien avant;
Et le plaisir la decevant
Tousjours l'emporte au gré de l'Onde:
BELLEGARDE les Matelots,   225
Jamais ne mesprisent les flots,
Quelque Phare qui leur éclaire:
Je feray mieux de relascher,
Et borner le soin de te plaire,
Par la crainte de te fascher.   230

XXIV   L'unique but où mon attente
Croit avoir raison d'aspirer,
C'est que tu vueilles m'asseurer
Que mon offrande te contente:
Donne m'en d'un clin de tes yeux   235
Un tesmoignage gracieux:
Et si tu la trouves petite,
Resouviens toy qu'une action
Ne peut avoir peu de merite,
Ayant beaucoup d'affection.   240

XXV   Ainsi de tant d'or et de soye,
Ton âge devide son cours,
Que tu reçoives tous les jours
Nouvelles matieres de joye:
Ainsi tes honneurs fleurissants   245
De jour en jour aillent croissants,
Malgré la fortune contraire:
Et ce qui les faict trébucher
De toy ny de TERMES ton frere,
Ne puisse jamais approcher.   250

> XXVI   Quand la faveur à pleines voiles,
> Tousjours compagne de vos pas,
> Vous feroit devant le trespas
> Avoir le front dans les Estoilles,
> Et remplir de vostre grandeur   255
> Ce que la terre a de rondeur:
> Sans estre menteur je puis dire
> Que jamais vos prosperitez
> N'iront jusques où je desire,
> Ny jusques où vous meritez. ²   260

* * *

Let us first consider the ode's themes and their progression as disclosed by Professor Wadsworth's analysis:

> Stanzas 1-6. The poet must break his long silence and, as the Muses urge him, immortalize Bellegarde in verse. But there is so much to praise; where to begin? 7-10. Bellegarde's great ancestors. But he is great in his own right too.... 11-22. Praise for Bellegarde. Everyone admires him (11). His service in escorting Marie de Médicis from Italy to France (12-13).... Comparison to Achilles (15-16), a transition leading to a description of Bellegarde's deeds of valor and loyal service to the throne (17-22). 23-26. The poet hopes that this poem will please Bellegarde and that Bellegarde (and his brother) will always be honored, although it will be impossible for him to be rewarded enough. ³

With the exception of the finale, the poem satisfies the norms of logical exposition. In the last three stanzas, however, there is an appearance of depleted inspiration, for as Professor Wadsworth states, "The poet simply announces, rather abruptly, that it is time to stop.... Then he descends to a conventional level of flattery for Bellegarde and for his brother, a person mentioned here for the first time." ⁴

Close inspection of the ode's non-argumentative strata dispels this impression of unconclusiveness and conventionality. From the

---

² Malherbe, I, pp. 99-107.
³ Wadsworth, p. 192.
⁴ Wadsworth, pp. 192-193.

metaphorical structures there emerge not only an unexpected identification of the brothers Bellegarde with a celebrated pair of mythological twins, but above all a complex system of stylistic features. Like that of the third completed ode, the style of the fourth serves to indicate links between the origin, nature, and rewards of the subjects' greatness. Moreover, for their complete sense, both patterns — allusive and stylistic — require the ode's logically questionable finale.

The Heroic Courtier

At first glance, it would appear that Malherbe sought to compare Bellegarde to Jason or to Achilles who, like the subject, were handsome and talented, and earned their place in history by valiance (cf. vv. 115-120, 141-160). For these explicit and rather decorative comparisons, however, there are no confirming details elsewhere in the text. One is then forced to inspect the poem's general motifs.

Bellegarde's ancestry provides the first indication:

> Si nommer en son parentage
> Une longue suitte d'ayeux,
> Que la gloire a mis dans les Cieux,
> Est reputé grand avantage:
> De qui n'est-il point reconnu,
> Que tousjours les tiens ont tenu
> Les charges les plus honorables,
> Dont le merite, et la raison,
> Quand les Destins sont favorables,
> Parent une Illustre maison?
>
> Qui ne sçait de quelles tempestes
> Leur fatale main autrefois,
> Portant la foudre de nos Rois,
> Des Alpes a battu les testes?
> Qui n'a veu dessous leurs combas,
> Le Pô mettre les cornes bas?
> Et les peuples de ses deux rives,
> Dans la frayeur ensevelis,
> Laisser leurs despoüilles captives
> A la mercy des Fleurs de Lis?   (vv. 61-80)

His family has attained eminence, splendor, and even immortality through military service to the French royal house. Secondly, Bellegarde possesses unusual proficiency in military skills, particularly horseback riding and jousting:

> Soit que l'honneur de la carriere
> T'appelle à monter à cheval,
> Soit qu'il se presente un rival
> Pour la lice, ou pour la barriere,
> Soit que tu donnes ton loisir
> A prendre quelque autre plaisir
> Esloigné des molles delices:
> Qui ne sçait que toute la Court
> A regarder tes exercices,
> Comme à des Theatres accourt?   (vv. 101-110)

Thirdly, a high point in his career was his escort of the future Queen on what proved a somewhat perilous journey to France:

> Quand tu passas en Italie,
> Où tu fus querir pour mon Roy
> Ce joyau d'honneur, et de foy,
> Dont l'Arne à la Seine s'allie:
> Thetis ne suivit-elle pas
> Ta bonne grace, et tes appas,
> Comme un object émerveillable.   (vv. 111-117)

Fourthly, he fought for the King, continuing the family tradition and fulfilling the promise contained in his impressive *exercices:*

> Depuis que pour sauver sa terre,
> Mon Roy, le plus grand des humains,
> Eut laissé partir de ses mains
> Le premier trait de son tonnerre,
> Jusqu'à la fin de ses exploits,
> Que tout eut reconnu ses lois,
> A t'il jamais défait armée,
> Pris ville, ny forcé rampart,
> Où ta valeur accoustumée
> N'ait eu la principale part?   (vv. 201-210)

Finally, Bellegarde received and maintained the poet, in which connection he is twice characterized as a goal or a guide to mariners:

> Belle-garde unique support
> Où mes vœux ont trouvé leur port. (vv. 5-6)

> BELLEGARDE les Matelots,
> Jamais ne mesprisent les flots,
> Quelque Phare qui leur éclaire. (vv. 225-227)

These qualities and actions recall no legendary prototype until the poet adds an important detail: the existence of another Bellegarde brother almost equal to the poet's patron. With that, an analogy emerges, likening the Bellegardes to a pair of mythological brothers. The children of Leda and Tyndareos, one became Sparta's leading horseman, while the other long retained its boxing championship; at a time of national peril, they brought a highly desirable young girl from foreign soil back to their own country (their sister Helen, who had been abducted by Theseus). They also served their city well in war, particularly against the Messenians. And ultimately, men came to recognize them not only as patrons of hospitality, but also — through what is now called Saint Elmo's fire — as protectors of sailors. They are, of course, Castor and Pollux. Confirming evidence appears in the final stanzas where the poet characteristically implies that the heros deserve nobler fate than that of Castor and Pollux, for they have surpassed their mythological counterparts. Castor, according to the most common versions of the myth, was killed in a quarrel which occurred during a cattle raid; to assure that the twins might never be separated, Zeus placed them both among the stars as the constellation Gemini. The Bellegardes, however, will not receive their just rewards until divine favor causes them

> ... devant le trespas
> Avoir le front dans les Estoilles,
> Et remplir de *[leur]* grandeur
> Ce que la terre a de rondeur. (vv. 253-256)

Malherbe's inclusion of the other Bellegarde brother is thus far from being conventional or gratuitous. Without that detail, the desired comparison between the duke and the Greek hero would have been almost insurmountably difficult. But if Bellegarde is so exceptional, why compare him to a mere hero? Surely a god was available. On considering the value system of the odes as an *œuvre*, it becomes clear that only the royal family may occupy the most exalted and illustrious ranks; their allies and instruments of policy (such as Bellegarde) — however admirable they may be — must occupy lower and less splendid positions. Castor — the athlete and patriotic soldier commanding real but perforce less intense admiration than a Theseus, a Venus, or a Hercules — is one of several ideal choices as an analogue for Bellegarde. That he additionally was a patron of hospitality made his selection inevitable.

A Pattern of Greatness

Embedded in the allusive framework of this ode is a tripartite stylistic system which characterizes the origin, nature, and reward of the Bellegarde excellence. Each constituent in this system is vitally related to the poem's finale.

i

Here, as in the two preceding odes, Malherbe indulges in a thematically significant pun. For the first and only time, however, he plays on the subject's own name.

An ode dedicated to Bellegarde necessarily has a "beau suject" (v. 2). Since — in Malherbe — like favors like, the Muses, "ces Beautez dont les appas / Ne sont que rigueurs" (vv. 16-17) will inspire only "agreables chansons" (v. 25) with respect to his virtues and actions. And well they might, since in seeking to describe Bellegarde's qualities, the poet is embarrassed by the richness from which he may choose; indeed, like a man gathering a bouquet, he is

> ... d'autant plus travaillé,
> Que le parterre est émaillé
> D'une diversité plus grande:
> Tant de fleurs de tant de costez,
> Faisant paroistre en leurs beautez
> L'artifice de la Nature. (vv. 42-47)

In all that Bellegarde does, he is more esthetically pleasing than the very practitioners of the conventional arts: when he rides and jousts, "Qui ne sçait que toute la Court / A regarder [ses] exercices, / Comme à des Theatres accourt?" (108-110); and when he escorted Marie de Médicis from Italy, "Thetis ne suivit-elle pas / Ta bonne grace, et tes appas, / Comme un object émerveillable?" (vv. 115-117). If the aggregate of Bellegarde's merits are so many beautiful flowers, it is only fitting that the acts they impel should win him "honneurs fleurissants" (v. 245). But Malherbe declares to Bellegarde that what he deserves but may never receive is to have "le front dans les Estoilles, / Et remplir de vostre grandeur / Ce que la terre a de rondeur" (vv. 254-256). Nothing less than occupation of and identification with an absolutely perfect form — this constitutes beauty as beauty's own reward.

ii

Embellishing the house of Bellegarde, the Destinies do not act upon a common race; indeed "[ils] parent une Illustre maison" (v. 70). In the same verse Malherbe links the idea of ornament to that of light. Light represents innate distinction, but also that which alone can justify it, the "rares qualitez, / Où brille un excez de lumiere" (vv. 56-57). These qualities in turn associate themselves with a pride which, unlike the moon, will not "luire d'un autre feu" (v. 90) than its own. By actions which follow from such splendid passions and dispositions, Bellegarde has put his "gloire en estime" (v. 177) and has also become a veritable "Phare" (v. 227) guiding other, lesser men (including the poet) through the darkness and tumult of the world. It is only appropriate, then, that at the end of his life Bellegarde's actions and their causes be translated from time to eternity, from earth to the Empyrean; thus Malherbe asserts Bellegarde's countenance should figure "dans les Estoilles" (v. 254).

iii

As in the two preceding odes, the hero's inner illumination pairs up inevitably with the image of verticality. Grandeur is the hallmark of the Bellegarde line: the subject's ancestors ascended indirectly, by bringing low the enemies of their King: their hand "des Alpes a battu les testes" (v. 74); and

> Qui n'a veu dessous leur combas,
> Le Pô mettre les cornes bas?
> Et les peuples de ses deux rives,
> Dans la frayeur ensevelis. (vv. 75-78)

For this, they were accorded the ultimate elevation: "la gloire [les] a mis dans les Cieux" (v. 63). Malherbe's host is himself marked by such "grandeur" (v. 255) that the "Muses hautaines" (v. 11) will not regard him as unworthy of an ode asserting that his countenance belongs "dans les Estoilles" (v. 254).

To this familiar pattern of grandeur and elevation, Malherbe adds a new image: the attainment of eminence while, like Atlas, bearing a heavy burden. The Bellegarde ancestors, for example, served France "portant la foudre de nos Rois" (v. 73). Bellegarde himself earned this ode, in part, as the "unique support" (v. 5) of the poet. Fittingly, one of his rewards is the admiration of the nation's finest hearts and minds, a prize which Envy sees him "emporter" (v. 95).

* * *

Thus the final stanza, already shown indispensable to the poem's allusive framework, draws its final and most conclusive justification from the combined requirements of poetic justice and stylistic consistency: the creation for Bellegarde of an emblem uniting beauty, elevation, and light.

VI

THE IDEA OF ORDER

Less than four months after Ravaillac's assassination of Henri IV, Malherbe began writing his fourth and briefest ode. Three months later, on December 23, 1610, he sent the final draft to his friend Peiresc. This is the last ode Malherbe was to complete before 1628, the year of his death.[1]

* * *

A LA REINE, SUR LES

HEUREUX SUCCEZ DE SA REGENCE

I   Nymphe qui jamais ne sommeilles,
    Et dont les messages divers
    En un moment sont aux oreilles
    Des peuples de tout l'Univers:
    Vole viste, et de la contree   5
    Par où le jour faict son entrée
    Jusqu'au rivage de Calis,
    Conte sur la terre et sur l'Onde,
    Que l'honneur unique du monde,
    C'est la Reine des fleurs de Lis.   10

---

[1] Malherbe, II, p. 32.

II   Quand son HENRY, de qui la gloire
Fut une merveille à nos yeux,
Loing des hommes s'en alla boire
Le nectar avecques les Dieux:
En ceste avanture effroyable,   15
A qui ne sembloit-il croyable,
Qu'on alloit voir une saison,
Où nos brutales perfidies
Feroient naistre des maladies
Qui n'auroient jamais guerison?   20

III   Qui ne pensoit que les Furies
Viendroient des abismes d'Enfer,
En de nouvelles barbaries
Employer la flamme et le fer?
Qu'un desbordement de licence,   25
Feroit souffrir à l'innocence
Toute sorte de cruautez?
Et que nos malheurs seroient pires,
Que nagueres sous les Busires
Que cét Hercule avoit dontez?   30

IV   Toutesfois depuis l'infortune
De cét abominable jour,
A peine la quatriesme Lune
Acheve de faire son tour:
Et la France a les destinées   35
Pour elle tellement tournées
Contre les vents seditieux,
Qu'au lieu de craindre la tempeste,
Il semble que jamais sa teste
Ne fut plus voisine des Cieux.   40

V   Au delà des bords de la Meuse,
L'Alemagne a veu nos guerriers,
Par une conqueste fameuse
Se couvrir le front de lauriers.
Tout a fléchy sous leur menace: 45
L'Aigle mesme leur a fait place:

>   Et les regardant approcher,
>   Comme Lyons à qui tout cede,
>   N'a point eu de meilleur remede,
>   Que de fuyr, et se cacher.

> VI   O Reine qui pleine de charmes
>   Pour toute sorte d'accidens,
>   As borné le flus de nos larmes
>   En ces miracles évidens:
>   Que peut la fortune publique
>   Te voüer d'assez magnifique,
>   Si mise au rang des immortels,
>   Dont ta vertu suit les exemples,
>   Tu n'as avec eux dans nos Temples,
>   Des Images, et des Autels?

> VII   Que sçauroit enseigner aux Princes
>   Le grand Demon qui les instruit,
>   Dont ta sagesse en nos Provinces
>   Chaque jour n'espande le fruit?
>   Et qui justement ne peut dire,
>   A te voir regir cét Empire,
>   Que si ton heur estoit pareil
>   A tes adorables merites,
>   Tu ferois dedans ses limites
>   Lever et coucher le Soleil?

> VIII   Le soin qui reste à nos pensées,
>   O bel Astre, c'est que tousjours
>   Nos felicitez commencées
>   Puissent continuer leur cours:
>   Tout nous rit, et nostre navire
>   A la bonace qu'il desire:
>   Mais si quelque injure du Sort
>   Provoquoit l'ire de Neptune,
>   Quel excez d'heureuse fortune,
>   Nous guarantiroit de la mort?

IX Assez de funestes batailles,
    Et de carnages inhumains
    Ont fait en nos propres entrailles
    Rougir nos desloyales mains:
    Donne ordre que sous ton Genie,   85
    Se termine ceste manie:
    Et que las de perpetuer
    Une si longue mal-veillance,
    Nous employons nostre vaillance
    Ailleurs qu'à nous entretuer.   90

X   La discorde aux crins de couleuvres,
    Peste fatale aux Potentats,
    Ne finit ses tragiques œuvres
    Qu'en la fin mesme des Estats:
    D'elle nasquit la frenesie   95
    De la Grece contre l'Asie:
    Et d'elle prindrent le flambeau
    Dont ils desolerent leur terre,
    Les deux freres de qui la guerre
    Ne cessa point dans le tombeau.   100

XI C'est en la paix que toutes choses
    Succedent selon nos desirs:
    Comme au Printemps naissent les roses,
    En la paix naissent les plaisirs:
    Elle met les pompes aux villes,   105
    Donne aux champs les moissons fertiles:
    Et de la Majesté des Lois
    Appuyant les pouvoirs suprémes,
    Fait demeurer les Diadémes
    Fermes sur la teste des Rois.   110

XII Ce sera dessous ceste Aegide,
    Qu'invincible de tous costez,
    Tu verras ces peuples sans bride
    Obeyr à tes volontez:
    Et surmontant leur esperance,   115
    Remettras en telle asseurance

Leur salut qui fut desploré,
Que vivre au siecle de Marie,
Sans mensonge et sans flatterie,
Sera vivre au siecle doré. 120

XIII Les Muses, les neuf belles Fees,
Dont les bois suivent les chansons,
Rempliront de nouveaux Orfées
La trouppe de leurs nourrissons:
Tous leurs vœux seront de te plaire: 125
Et si ta faveur tutelaire
Fait signe de les avoüer,
Jamais ne partit de leurs veilles
Rien qui se compare aux merveilles
Qu'elles feront pour te loüer. 130

XIV En ceste hautaine entreprise,
Commune à tous les beaux Esprits,
Plus ardant qu'un Athlete à Pise,
Je me feray quitter le pris:
Et quand j'auray peint ton image, 135
Quiconque verra mon ouvrage,
Avoûra que Fontaine-bleau,
Le Louvre, ny les Tuileries,
En leurs superbes galeries
N'ont point un si riche tableau. 140

XV Apollon à portes ouvertes
Laisse indifferemment cueillir
Les belles fueilles tousjours vertes
Qui gardent les noms de vieillir:
Mais l'Art d'en faire les Couronnes, 145
N'est pas sçeu de toutes personnes.
Et trois ou quatre seulement,
Au nombre desquels on me range,
Peuvent donner une loüange
Qui demeure eternellement.[2] 150

* * *

---

[2] Malherbe, I, pp. 87-92.

With respect to logical unity, Professor Wadsworth has no remark to make on this poem. The key to its structure, he asserts, is the "give-and-take development, or argument and rebuttal, so characteristic of Malherbe's art." [3] This form of exposition gives rise to the following order of themes:

> Stanzas 1-3. The poet states his intention [to praise Marie], then expresses fear for public misfortunes, following the assassination of Henri IV. 4-8. But these fears were groundless; France is strong and thriving. Praise for Marie's accomplishments. Transition (8) to other possible dangers. 9-12. Hope expressed that war and discord can be avoided, that her reign will be a Golden Age. 13-15. Then the Muses will praise her. Above all, Malherbe will honor her and make her immortal. [4]

Inspection of the ode's allusions and style will show, however, that beyond the tight dialectic of its argumentation the ode attains a highly poetic integration.

The Light of the East

The Queen is no ordinary creature, but a "bel Astre" (v. 72) whose exalted and luminous presence can invoke supernatural "charmes / Pour toute sorte d'accidens" (vv. 51-52). Since, in Malherbe, like attracts like, the Queen married "HENRY, de qui la gloire / Fut une merveille à nos yeux" (vv. 11-12). As a result of an "avanture effroyable" (v. 15), the King "loing des hommes s'en alla boire / Le nectar avecques les Dieux" (vv. 13-14). The Queen has thus been put in the King's place, and she must now "regir cét Empire" (v. 66). That she is intellectually competent to perform the King's tasks Malherbe implies when he asks rhetorically:

> Que sçauroit enseigner aux Princes
> Le grand Demon qui les instruit,
> Dont ta sagesse en nos Provinces
> Chaque jour n'espande le fruit?   (vv. 61-64)

---

[3] Wadsworth, p. 193.
[4] *Ibid.*

That her personality will command deference, the poet has no doubt, for he predicts:

> Ce sera dessous ceste Aegide,
> Qu'invincible de tous costez,
> Tu verras ces peuples sans bride
> Obeyr à tes volontez.   (vv. 111-114)

Furthermore, one need not fear that the Queen will avoid military undertakings when the national interest is at stake:

> Au delà des bords de la Meuse,
> L'Alemagne a veu nos guerriers,
> Par une conqueste fameuse
> Se couvrir le front de lauriers.
> Tout a fléchy sous leur menace:
> L'Aigle mesme leur a fait place:
> Et les regardant approcher,
> Comme Lyons à qui tout cede,
> N'a point eu de meilleur remede,
> Que de fuyr, et se cacher.   (vv. 41-50)

(Malherbe refers, of course, to the taking of Juliers, by French forces on September 1, 1610.) Order, so long threatened from within by old Ligueurs and dissident Protestants, will soon be restored and thanks to that restoration, a stable civilization will flourish:

> C'est en la paix que toutes choses
> Succedent selon nos desirs:
> Comme au Printemps naissent les roses,
> En la paix naissent les plaisirs:
> Elle met les pompes aux villes,
> Donne aux champs les moissons fertilles:
> Et de la Majesté des Lois
> Appuyant les pouvoirs suprémes,
> Fait demeurer les Diadémes
> Fermes sur la teste des Rois.   (vv. 101-110)

Marie's superhuman excellence — like that of Henri IV — deserves reward in kind. Malherbe twice reveals the precise character of that reward. Just as the loftiness of Henri IV — that latter-day Hercules — won him assumption into heaven, so the goddess-like merit of the Queen requires deification:

> Que peut la fortune publique
> Te voüer d'assez magnifique,
> Si mise au rang des immortels,
> Dont ta vertu suit les exemples,
> Tu n'as avec eux dans nos Temples,
> Des Images, et des Autels? (vv. 55-60)

Moreover, because her special office is to regulate the movements of an Empire, she will be well suited to make "dedans ses limites / Lever et coucher le Soleil" (vv. 69-70).

To sum up, Marie's career consists of the following motifs: a beautiful and superhuman woman; her marriage to a great king; his premature death; her service as regent, including foreign conquest and the promise of improvement in the general level of civilization; and finally, her apotheosis. These motifs recall the career of antiquity's greatest Queen: the daughter of the sea-goddess Derceto of Ascalon, she married Ninus, founder of Nineveh and conquerer of Asia; as Ninus's widow, and as regent for their son Ninyas, she conquered Egypt and Ethiopia, built Babylon and, above all, the hanging gardens of Media; after a reign of forty-two years, she was turned into a dove and worshiped as a deity. This Assyrian Queen is none other than Semiramis, well-known to the Renaissance by references in Herodotus, Ovid's *Metamophoses* and *Amores*, as well as Lucian's *Dialogues*.

By implication, Malherbe's Marie surpasses Semiramis. Marie is apparently devoid of the lubricity that Ovid attributes to her mythological counterpart. In addition, Marie is clearly innocent of her husband's death, while Semiramis was suspected of assassinating Ninus. But the poet leads the reader to expect more of the poem than this intriguing analogy. He states that the Queen's excellence as regent will be taught as an example to princes. And to show what this excellence includes, Malherbe embedded in his narrative an elaborate system of significant stylistic features.

A Syllabus of Perfection

The single notion controlling the ode's style is that of regency itself. The radical appears twice: once in the title, which wishes Marie success in her *Régence;* and once in the text, where the poet speaks of seeing Marie "regir cét Empire" (v. 66). The sense that Malherbe attaches to the word includes but goes beyond the common definition, that is, "to rule in another's stead." Malherbe also recalls the etymological meaning, "to impose order and value."

Regency appears here as the affirmation of norms which are expressed in spatial terms. Moral or political authority in this ode, as in the third and fourth, is indistinguishable from imagery of dimensional extremes, usually vertical. Thus when France survives a storm of seditious threats after the assassination of Henri IV, "il semble que jamais sa teste / Ne fut plus voisine des Cieux" (39-40). Similarly, when Marie's army took Juliers from the Empire, and thus removed a threat to French interests, the nation gained stature, at least indirectly, by bending an external enemy. In the same stanza Malherbe re-expresses the same idea in terms of a horizontal relationship — France takes precedence over the German emperor's eagle:

> Tout a fléchy sous leur menace:
> L'Aigle mesme leur a fait place.   (vv. 45-46)

The only object capable of overtopping the Queen or her appointed agents in war is a symbol of her own eminence — the wreath of laurels (v. 44), the "Diadéme" (v. 109), or the "Couronnes" (v. 145) fashioned, of course, by the poet himself.

Whereas the regent — in her relations with external rivals — must positively assert her own superiority and precedence by bringing them low and by making them yield to her, she observes very different spatial norms and resorts to very different strategies when dealing with internal enemies, whether moral or physical, natural or supernatural. In this connection, the third and fourth stanzas are of particular interest:

> Qui ne pensoit que les Furies
> Viendroient des abismes d'Enfer,
> En de nouvelles barbaries
> Employer la flamme et le fer?
> Qu'un desbordement de licence,
> Feroit souffrir à l'innocence
> Toute sorte de cruautez?
> Et que nos malheurs seroient pires,

> Que nagueres sous les Busires
> Que cét Hercule avoit dontez?
>
> Toutefois depuis l'infortune
> De cét abominable jour,
> A peine la quatriesme Lune
> Acheve de faire son tour:
> Et la France a les destinées
> Pour elle tellement tournées
> Contre les vents seditieux,
> Qu'au lieu de craindre la tempeste,
> Il semble que jamais sa teste
> Ne fut plus voisine des Cieux.   (vv. 21-40)

The first of these stanzas describes the moral and political dangers expected to threaten France after the murder of Henri IV. In each case, the danger involves the violation of a norm expressed in spatial terms: the destructive emergence of the Furies from their accustomed enclosure in Hell, and the overflow of cruelty, revenge and ambition from their usual confinement. The poet implies that the Queen literally repressed these entities and — aided by destiny — preserved order. In the second of these stanzas, Malherbe describes potential disorder as a storm battering an objective. The winds are "seditieux" in the sense that they defy the limits of force and velocity imposed upon them by nature. Since they cannot be cut off at the point of origin, France standing firm resists the horizontal assault at the point of impact, until the winds finally deplete themselves.

The scope of this ode's spatial imagery includes the Regent's loyal subjects and her adversaries. In the face of internal sedition, and foreign threats to the nation's safety, there is a danger of terror and finally despair. Thus, by humiliating some opponents, by containing others, and by exhausting still others by resistance, the Regent has magically "borné le flus de nos larmes" (v. 53), that is, by inaugurating an age of security, she has fully averted a tragic eruption of grief.

Malherbe's characterization of Marie's reign also includes an image of desirable movement through space:

> Le soin qui reste à nos pensées,
> O bel Astre, c'est que tousjours
> Nos felicitez commencées

> Puissent continuer leur cours:
> Tout nous rit, et nostre navire
> A la bonace qu'il desire. (vv. 71-76)

A ship which, having left port and set its course, proceeds with speed and stability toward its goal, represents the norm. Corresponding to its balance and security must be the internal harmony of the passengers:

> Assez de funestes batailles,
> Et de carnages inhumains
> Ont fait en nos propres entrailles
> Rougir nos desloyales mains:
> Donne ordre que sous ton Genie,
> Se termine ceste manie. (vv. 81-86)

Paradoxically, the outcome of Marie's efforts in the domain of space will be a felicitous departure from order in the domain of time. France will achieve such a degree of political and social perfection that the ages of man will reverse themselves. Hence, as desired in the second ode, "vivre au siecle de Marie / ... / Sera vivre au siecle doré" (vv. 118 and 120). Thanks to Malherbe, she will also receive the reward appropriate to her efforts: celebrity that knows no limit, either in space — for his poem will resound "aux oreilles / Des peuples de tout l'Univers" (vv. 3-4) — or in time — for Malherbe is one of the three or four who "peuvent donner une loüange / Qui demeure eternellement" (vv. 149-150).[5]

---

[5] For an important historical and philosophical treatment of themes discussed in this chapter, see Professor Maria A. Green's unpublished Ph.D. dissertation, *Sovereign Power and Sovereign Glory: A Study of the Influence of Jean Bodin's Political Ideas on Malherbe*, University of Washington, 1969.

VII

THE FIRST SUBJECT OF THE REALM

In 1614 — four years after completing the fifth ode — Malherbe began writing a sixth, "Pour la Reine mere du Roy pendant sa Regence." For various technical reasons, suggested in the Appendix, the poet abandoned that ode without having brought it to completion. He did not, in fact, undertake a major lyric work for thirteen years, when, between July 1627 and March 1628, he wrote his last completed ode.[1] Of the historical events lying behind this ode, Professor Fromilhague has written:

> La Rochelle, "place de sûreté" des protestants, foyer de résistance à l'autorité de Louis XIII et de Richelieu, fut assiégée par l'armée royale en 1627. Le roi, parti de Paris le 20 juin, mais tombé malade en route, n'arriva au camp que le 12 octobre, accompagné de son ministre. Dans l'intervalle, le 22 juillet, les Anglais, venus au secours des assiégés, avaient débarqué dans l'île de Ré. Ils en furent chassés le 8 novembre. Mais La Rochelle ne devait capituler qu'un an après, le 29 octobre 1628.[2]

* * *

---

[1] Malherbe, II, p. 86.
[2] Malherbe, II, p. 85.

POUR LE ROY

ALLANT CHASTIER LA REBELLION DES ROCHELOIS, ET CHASSER LES ANGLOIS, QUI EN LEUR FAVEUR ESTOIENT DESCENDUS EN L'ISLE DE RÉ

I   Donq un nouveau labeur à tes armes s'appreste:
Pren ta foudre, LOUYS, et va comm' un Lion
Donner le dernier coup à la derniere teste
    De la rebellion.   4

II   Fay choir en sacrifice au Demon de la France
Les fronts trop eslevez de ces ames d'Enfer:
Et n'espargne contr'eux pour notre delivrance
    Ny le feu ny le fer.   8

III   Assez de leurs complots l'infidelle malice
A nourry le desordre et la sedition.
Quitte le nom de JUSTE, ou fay voir ta Justice
    En leur punition.   12

IV   Le centiesme Decembre a les plaines ternies,
Et le centiesme Avril les a peintes de fleurs:
Depuis que parmy nous brutales manies
    Ne causent que des pleurs.   16

V   Dans toutes les fureurs des siecles de tes Peres
Les monstres les plus noirs firent ils jamais rien,
Que l'inhumanité de ces cueurs de viperes
    Ne renouvelle au tien?   20

VI   Par qui sont aujourd'huy tant de villes desertes?
Tant de grans bastimens en masures changez?
Et de tant de chardons les campagnes couvertes
    Que par ces enragez?   24

VII Les Sceptres devant eux n'ont point de privileges:
　　　Les Immortels eux mesme en sont persecutez:
　　　Et c'est aux plus saints lieux que leurs mains sacrileges
　　　　　Font plus d'impietez.　　　　　　　　　　　28

VIII Marche, va les destruire: esteins-en la semence:
　　　Et suy jusqu'à leur fin ton courroux genereux,
　　　Sans jamais escouter ny pitié ni clemence
　　　　　Qui te parle pour eux.　　　　　　　　　32

IX Ils ont beau vers le Ciel leurs murailles accroistre:
　　　Beau d'un soin assidu travailler à leurs Forts:
　　　Et creuzer leurs fossez jusqu'à faire paroistre
　　　　　Le jour entre les morts.　　　　　　　　36

X   Laisse les esperer, laisse les entreprendre:
　　　Il suffit que ta cause est la cause de DIEU:
　　　Et qu'avecque ton bras ell'a pour la deffendre
　　　　　Les soings de Richelieu.　　　　　　　　40

XI Richelieu ce Prelat, de qui toute l'envie
　　　Est de voir ta grandeur aux Indes se borner:
　　　Et qui visiblement ne fait cas de sa vie
　　　　　Que pour te la donner.　　　　　　　　　44

XII Rien que ton interest n'occupe sa pensée:
　　　Nuls divertissemens ne l'appellent ailleurs:
　　　Et de quelques bons yeux qu'on ait vanté Lyncée,
　　　　　Il en a de meilleurs.　　　　　　　　　　48

XIII Son ame toute grande est une ame hardie,
　　　Qui pratique si bien l'art de nous secourir,
　　　Que pourveu qu'il soit creu, nous n'avons maladie,
　　　　　Qu'il ne sçache guerir.　　　　　　　　　52

XIV Le Ciel qui doit le bien selon qu'on le merite,
　　　Si de ce grand Oracle il ne t'eust assisté,
　　　Par un autre present n'eust jamais esté quitte
　　　　　Envers ta pieté.　　　　　　　　　　　　56

XV Va, ne differe plus tes bonnes Destinées:
    Mon Apollon t'asseure, et t'engage sa foy,
    Qu'employant ce Tiphys, Syrtes et Cyanées
        Seront havres pour toy.   60

XVI Certes, ou je me trompe, ou desja la Victoire,
     Qui son plus grand honneur de tes palmes attent,
     Est aux bors de Charante en son habit de gloire
         Pour te rendre content.   64

XVII Je la voy qui t'appelle, et qui semble te dire:
      Roy, le plus grand des Rois, et qui m'es le plus cher,
      Si tu veux que je t'aide à sauver ton Empire,
          Il est temps de marcher.   68

XVIII Que sa façon est brave, et sa mine asseurée!
       Qu'elle a fait richement son armure estoffer!
       Et qu'il se connoist bien à la voir si parée
           Que tu vas triompher!   72

XIX Telle en ce grand assaut, où des fils de la Terre
     La rage ambitieuse à leur honte parut,
     Elle sauva le Ciel, et rua le tonnerre
         Dont Briare mourut.   76

XX Desja de tous costez s'avançoient les approches:
    Icy couroit Mimas; là Typhon se battoit;
    Et là suoit Euryte à détacher les roches
        Qu'Encelade jettoit.   80

XXI A peine ceste Vierge eut l'affaire embrassée,
     Qu'aussi tost Jupiter en son Trosne remis,
     Vit selon son desir la tempeste cessée,
         Et n'eust plus d'ennemis.   84

XXII Ces Colosses d'orgueil furent tous mis en poudre,
      Et tous couverts des monts qu'ils avoient arrachez:
      Phlegre qui les receut, pût encore la foudre
          Dont ils furent touchez.   88

XXIII L'exemple de leur race à jamais abolie
 Devoit sous ta mercy tes rebelles ployer:
 Mais seroit ce raison qu'une mesme folie
  N'eust pas mesme loyer? 92

XXIV Desja l'estonnement leur fait la couleur blesme:
 Et ce lasche voisin qu'ils sont allé querir,
 Miserable qu'il est, se condamne luy mesme
  A fuyr ou mourir. 96

XXV Sa faute le remord: Megere le regarde:
 Et luy porte l'esprit à ce vray sentiment,
 Que d'une injuste offense il aura, quoy qu'il tarde,
  Le juste chastiment. 100

XXVI Bien semble estre la mer une barre assez forte
 Pour nous oster l'espoir qu'il puisse estre battu:
 Mais est il rien de clos dont ne t'ouvre la porte
  Ton heur et ta vertu? 104

XXVII Neptune importuné de ses voiles infames,
 Comme tu parestras au passage des flots,
 Voudra que ses Tritons mettent la main aux rames,
  Et soient tes matelots. 108

XXVIII Là rendront tes guerriers tant de sortes de preuves,
 Et d'une telle ardeur pousseront leurs efforts,
 Que le sang estranger fera monter nos fleuves
  Au dessus de leurs bords. 112

XXIX Par cest exploit fatal en tous lieux va renaistre
 La bonne opinion des courages François:
 Et le monde croira, s'il doit avoir un maistre,
  Qu'il faut que tu le sois. 116

XXX O que pour avoir part en si belle avanture
 Je me souhaiterois la fortune d'Eson,
 Qui, vieil comme je suis, revint contre Nature
  En sa jeune saison! 120

XXXI De quel peril extreme est la guerre suivie,
 Où je ne fisse voir que tout l'Or du Levant
 N'a rien que je compare aux honneurs d'une vie
  Perduë en te servant? 124

XXXII Toutes les autres morts n'ont merite ny marque:
 Celle cy porte seule un éclat radieux
 Qui fait revivre l'homme, et le met de la barque
  A la table des Dieux. 128

XXXIII Mais quoy? tous les pensers dont les ames bien nées
 Excitent leur valeur, et flattent leur devoir,
 Que sont ce que regrets, quand le nombre d'années
  Leur oste le pouvoir? 132

XXXIV Ceux à qui la chaleur ne bout plus dans les veines
 En vain dans les combats ont des soins diligens:
 Mars est comme l'Amour: ses travaux et ses peines
  Veulent de jeunes gens. 136

XXXV Je suis vaincu du temps: je cede à ses outrages:
 Mon esprit seulement exempt de sa rigueur,
 A de quoy tesmoigner en ses derniers ouvrages
  Sa premiere vigueur. 140

XXXVI Les puissantes faveurs dont Parnasse m'honore,
 Non loin de mon berceau commencerent leur cours:
 Je les posseday jeune; et les possede encore
  A la fin de mes jours. 144

XXXVII Ce que j'en ay receu, je veux te le produire:
 Tu verras mon addresse; et ton front ceste fois
 Sera ceint de rayons qu'on ne vit jamais luire
  Sur la teste des Rois. 148

XXXVIII Soit que de tes lauriers ma lyre s'entretienne,
 Soit que de tes bontez je la face parler:
 Quel rival assez vain pretendra que la sienne
  Ait dequoy m'égaler? 152

XXXIX Le fameux Amphion, dont la voix nompareille,
Bastissant une ville estonna l'Univers,
Quelque bruit qu'il ait eu, n'a point fait de merveille
   Que ne facent mes vers.   156

XL Par eux de tes beaux faits la terre sera pleine:
Et les peuples du Nil, qui les auront ouys,
Donneront de l'encens, comme ceux de la Seine,
   Aux autels de LOUYS.   160

* * *

"This ode reveals considerable attention to problems of structure,"[3] wrote Professor Wadsworth, who summarized as follows the topics and their arrangement:

> Stanzas 1-9. Exhortation to the King to slay the Protestants because of the crimes and wars they have engendered. 10. Transition. 11-14. Praise for the King's great minister, Richelieu. 15. Transition. 16-29. Predictions of victory. Examples from mythology (16-22). Fears of the enemy and their English allies (23-25). Neptune will also help (26-29). 30-40. Malherbe's own feelings. He wishes he could take part in this war (30-32) but he is too old (33-34). Transition; his mind is still vigorous (35). His poetic gifts are still unmatched, and he will use them to spread the glory of Louis XIII (36-40).[4]

In fact, Professor Wadsworth finds only one digression, "i.e., the eulogy of Richelieu [which] had to be included, for professional and political reasons," but "it is carefully bracketed in transitional stanzas."[5] This apparently fragmentary portrait is, like all other logically questionable portions of Malherbe's completed odes, an integral part of the poem's pattern of comparisons.

---

[3] Malherbe, I, pp. 166-171.
[4] Wadsworth, p. 194.
[5] *Ibid.*

A Many-Splendored King

The first twenty-nine stanzas deal with the King himself, with his allies, and with the Protestant rebels. Rather than follow his usual, circuitous practice Malherbe directly draws comparisons with three or four distinct myths, both pagan and Christian.

In the first instance, Malherbe identifies the King with Hercules, the hero he had habitually identified with Henri IV:

> Donq un nouveau labeur à tes armes s'appreste:
> Pren ta foudre, LOUYS, et va comm' un Lion
> Donner le dernier coup à la derniere teste
>   De la rebellion.
>
> Fay choir en sacrifice au Demon de la France
> Les fronts trop eslevez de ces ames d'Enfer:
> Et n'espargne contr'eux pour notre delivrance
>   Ny le feu ny le fer.
>   (vv. 1-8)

The Protestant rebels are to the King what Hydra was to Hercules; and their effect on France — the sense of which will figure importantly in the next section — is nothing less than catastrophic:

> Par qui sont aujourd'huy tant de villes desertes?
> Tant de grans bastimens en masures changez?
> Et de tant de chardons les campagnes couvertes
>   Que par ces enragez?
>
> Les Sceptres devant eux n'ont point de privileges:
> Les Immortels eux mesme en sont persecutez:
> Et c'est aux plus saints lieux que leurs mains
>   [sacrileges
>   Font plus d'impietez.
>   (vv. 21-28)

They must be destroyed.

In the second instance, Malherbe makes what appears to be the only Biblical allusion in the six completed odes:

> Ils ont beau vers le Ciel leurs murailles accroistre:
> Beau d'un soin assidu travailler à leur Forts:
> Et creuzer leurs fossez jusqu'à faire paroistre
>   Le jour entre les morts.
>
> Laisse les esperer, laisse les entreprendre:
> Il suffit que ta cause est la cause de DIEU.
>   (vv. 33-38)

The walls of la Rochelle are perhaps those of Jericho; if so, Louis XIII is Joshua. Thus, unless the city capitulates before the King lays siege in God's own name, the walls may miraculously fall.

In the third instance, the reference is long and complex. The King is aided by Richelieu:

> ... ce Prelat, de qui toute l'envie
> Est de voir ta grandeur aux Indes se borner:
> Et qui visiblement ne fait cas de sa vie
>   Que pour te la donner.
>
> Rien que ton interest n'occupe sa pensée:
> Nuls divertissemens ne l'appelent ailleurs.
>   (vv. 41-46)

And to the prime minister the poet attributes the greatest perspicacity:

> Et de quelques bons yeux qu'on ait vanté Lyncée,
>   Il en a de meilleurs.
>   (vv. 47-48)

Indeed Richelieu is like a perfected Lynceus and the King's other subordinates resemble the other Argonauts:

> Va, ne differe plus tes bonnes Destinées:
> Mon Apollon t'asseure, et t'engage sa foy,
> Qu'employant ce Tiphys, Syrtes et Cyanées
>   Seront havres pour toy.
>   (vv. 57-60)

The King must then be analogous to Jason, while the Protestants are perhaps the dragon that guards the fleece; the "habit de gloire" (v. 63) worn by Victory, may thus represent Louis XIII's rightful hegemony over France.

The final instance — already used in the second completed ode — pertains to the Giants who sought to cast Jupiter down from Olympus; their efforts, it will be remembered, were frustrated by Fate (here, "Victoire" [v. 61]):

> Telle en ce grand assaut, où des fils de la Terre
> La rage ambitieuse à leur honte parut,
> Elle sauva le Ciel, et rua le tonnerre
>   Dont Briare mourut.
>
> Desja de tous costez s'avançoient les approches:
> Icy couroit Mimas; là Typhon se battoit;
> Et là suoit Euryte à détacher les roches
>   Qu'Encelade jettoit.
>
> A peine ceste Vierge eut l'affaire embrassée,
> Qu'aussi tost Jupiter en son Trosne remis,
> Vit selon son desir la tempeste cessée,
>   Et n'eust plus d'ennemis.
>   (vv. 73-84)

The analogy is plain: Louis XIII is to the Protestants what Zeus was to the Giants.

This series of mythological references may appear to be a mere assortment of comparisons which serve to place the action into an epic perspective, for their essential interrelation — to say nothing of their connection with the poet's more personal expression in the poem's last nineteen stanzas — is far from explicit. Examination of the style, however, discloses subtle links, some of them familiar — owing to the poet's predeliction for certain images and puns — others less so — because of the poet's continuing creativity.

Unity in Variety

An in previous poems, Malherbe here links elevation with value. Likened to Hercules, the King uses the weapon of Zeus, "foudre" (v. 2); the King himself is "le plus grand des Rois" (v. 66); like Jason, he receives as reward for military achievement the "palmes" (v. 62) which augment his stature. As before, the King's enemies are base: like the heads of the Hydra, those "ames d'Enfer" (v. 6), the Protestants are also arrogant and aspire too high: they have "les fronts trop eslevez" (v. 6). Their calamitous effect upon the kingdom consists, in part, of having debased what should be exalted: thus are "grans bastimens en masures changez" (v. 22); thus "c'est aux plus saints lieux que leurs mains sacrileges / Font plus d'impietez" (vv. 27-28); thus "les Sceptres devant eux n'ont point de privileges" (v. 25). In the character of Jericho's builders, they have erected walls "vers le Ciel" (v. 33). As Giants, they are "fils de la Terre" (v. 73) and "Colosses d'orgueil" (v. 85) who make a "grand assaut" (v. 73) — in the root sense of a "leap upward" — against divine authority. The King, as Hercules, is thus urged to make the Hydra heads "choir en sacrifice au Demon de la France" (v. 5) and "les destruire" (v. 29), the latter in its etymological sense, "to pull down." By implication, of course, the walls of La Rochelle, like those of Jericho, will fall flat if the city does not surrender. As Giants, the Protestant rebels will deservedly fall beneath the "tonnerre" (v. 75) that Victory will hurl at them. And, "couverts des monts" (v. 86), they will be crushed — "tous mis en poudre" (v. 85) — and permanently held down.

The imagery of light and darkness also plays its familiar role. The King's affiliation with light stems from the "foudre" (v. 2) that he wields as a Zeus-like Hercules, the "gloire" (v. 63) that will receive as Jason, and the "Ciel" (v. 75) that he occupies as Zeus. Richelieu, the new Lynceus, is implicitly associated with light, for his special gift of perspicacity suggests the image of *clartés*. The Hydra heads are "les monstres les plus noirs" (v. 18) come from the darkness of "Enfer" (v. 6), and the Giants are "fils de la Terre" (v. 73).

To these familiar patterns Malherbe adds two that are novel: the antithesis of plenum and void, linked in certain passages with that of order and disorder. The catastrophic effect of the Hydra's "brutales manies" (v. 15) is double: first, the abnormal emptiness of cities — "Par qui sont aujourd'huy tant de villes desertes?" (v. 21); and secondly, the abnormal state of the fields, now empty of wheat, and "de tant de chardons ... couvertes" (v. 23). A similar disorder occurs when the Giants disturb nature by ripping mountains up and dislodging rocks to hurl at Olympus. With order restored, Zeus "en son Trosne remis" (v. 82), and the Hydra finally put down, Malherbe implies that the cities will fill with people, the fields with wheat, and the world with the King's eminence. This detail marks the province of Richelieu "de qui toute l'envie / Est de voir ta grandeur aux Indes se borner" (vv. 41-42).

To sum up, then, the four seemingly disjunct mythological references are in fact tightly interwoven by style which unites royal interest and accomplishments with luminosity, elevation, order and the plenum, while affiliating the interests and deeds of the Protestants with darkness, abasement of the lofty, the rise of what ought to lie hidden, the emptying of what ought to remain full, and the definition of what ought to be limitless. Up to this point, however, the best the King's human allies can do is offer perspicacious advice, pious wishes, and physical involvement with an expansion of royal glory. His superhuman ally is also limited. Although Victory wins specific battles for the King, helps him acquire the fleece of absolute rule and crush the Giants, she assures nothing for the long-term.

The Self-Acknowledged Legislator of the World

The following eleven stanzas express more than the poet's regret at being too old to help the King except as a propagandist in verse. These stanzas are, in fact, the most paradoxical and self-assertive of the malherbian canon.

The section begins with a declaration of weakness. Malherbe states that "vieil comme je suis ... vaincu du temps: /je cede à ses outrages" (vv. 119, 137). Indeed, "le nombre d'années" (v. 131) have emptied the poet of his physical powers. Though supporting the monarch, he cannot emulate the vigorous, purposeful action that he urges upon Louis XIII, e.g.:

>   Pren ta foudre, LOUYS, et va comm' un Lion
>   (v. 2)

>   Marche, va les destruire   (v. 29)

As the poet is excluded from the possibility of fighting for the King, he is also seemingly excluded from rewards reserved to those of the King's soldiers who die in battle: a burst of light, and elevation:

> Toutes les autres morts n'ont merite ny marque:
> Celle cy porte seule un éclat radieux
> Qui fait revivre l'homme, et le met de la barque
>   A la table des Dieux.
>   (vv. 125-128)

It would in fact appear that Malherbe resembles Richelieu, since neither can act and both are merely right-minded and perspicacious.

Over against this weakness is an opposite and more-than-equal strength, for though the body has been conquered by time,

> Mon esprit seulement exempt de sa rigueur,
> A de quoy tesmoigner en ses derniers ouvrages
>   Sa premiere vigueur.
>
> Les puissantes faveurs dont Parnasse m'honore,
> Non loin de mon berceau commencerent leurs cours:
> Je les posseday jeune; et les possede encore
>   A la fin de mes jours.
>
> Ce que j'en ay receu, je veux te le produire:
> Tu verras mon addresse.
>   (vv. 138-146)

If victory can bring the King only a crown of "palmes" (v. 62), which increases his stature but not his radiance, the poet by his verses will remedy this lack:

> ... et ton front ceste fois
> Sera ceint de rayons qu'on ne vit jamais luire
>   Sur la teste des Rois.
>   (vv. 146-148)

Indeed, the poet will go further. He will deify the King, and assure that his image is eternally worshipped. Whereas Richelieu and the gods erect nothing in the King's honor and the other subjects arrogantly draw themselves up to challenge his authority, the poet, a creative genius, surpassing even Amphion, erects an awesome structure — a verbal monument to the King's greatness:

> Le fameux Amphion, dont la voix nompareille,
> Bastissant une ville estonna l'Univers,
> Quelque bruit qu'il ait eu, n'a point fait de merveille
> Que ne facent mes vers.
> (vv. 153-156)

Finally he poet will achieve what Richelieu only hoped to do, fill the known world with the King's glory and grandeur: by his verse

> ... de tes beaux faits la terre sera pleine:
> (v. 157)

And by this act, Malherbe will enable the King to become what poets had merely compared him to, a god:

> Et les peuples du Nil, qui les auront ouys,
> Donneront de l'encens, comme ceux de la Seine,
> Aux autels de LOUYS.
> (vv. 158-160)

Thus the poet establishes himself as the King's greatest — that is, most powerful and efficacious — subject and, paradoxically, his most generous patron.

VIII

FROM COHERENCE TO JUDGMENT

Thus far, this work has made only limited reference to the general principles of structure and the historical pattern of technical development in Malherbe's six completed odes. These questions require, and will now receive, fuller treatment.

At the outset it should be noted that an inventory of the structural elements contained in all six poems would — within the present set of assumptions — distinguish between two classes: literal and figurative. The former includes the "successions de faits" from whose less-than-rigorous presentation stems the surface disorder noted by Professor Wadsworth. The latter class contains the techniques by means of which Malherbe integrated the fragmentary literal elements into an "ordre supérieur et caché." Admittedly, this distinction is artificial, since each set of elements depends very heavily upon the other for its value in the context of any given ode; they are here separated only for the sake of clarity.

"... les successions de faits..."

On the literal level, the malherbian ode is a versified discourse containing narrative, rhetorical, descriptive, and lyric features, combining from two to seven of the following topics:

1. *Praise* for the moral, intellectual, esthetic, and even athletic qualities of the subject (including, whenever appropriate, his ancestors and immediate family) and for the past,

present, or future acts permitted by these qualities in the domains of politics, war, religion, and society; brief explicit comparisons between the subject and mythological personages or natural phenomena.

2. *Condemnation* of the defects and actions of the subject's rivals or enemies, unless converted to instruments of royal policy.

3. *Sympathetic portrayal* of the subject's well-meaning but materially or intellectually limited allies and dependents.

4. *Exhortations or questions* urging upon the subject or on his divine patrons certain courses of action in the interest of the realm.

5. *Prediction* of future actions or conditions.

6. *Assertions* concerning the power of poetry — particularly Malherbe's — to confer upon the subject the verbal equivalent of his just but unattainable rewards.

"*l'ordre supérieur et caché*"

On the figurative level, the poet establishes in every ode one or more of the following implicit comparisons, which enfold all of the literal facts.

1. *Allusion.* The poet models the action and its moral or intellectual causes on certain unparticularized motifs of a single mythological pattern; this expedient serves to enhance the subject's value by comparing him to the protagonist in an epic or cosmic event. The poet may also invert, conditionally or unconditionally, any motif in the model which relates to the protagonist's disgrace, crime, or tragic flaw; this expedient serves further to enhance the poet's praise of his subject by demonstrating the latter's superiority to his legendary counterpart.

2. *Style*. The poet establishes systems of images, metonymies, repeated key words and their synonyms, as well as verbal ambiguities (including etymological puns, and equivocations on abstract and concrete senses). These systems liken the agents — their qualities, actions, and rewards — to essences, states, characters, and relations which have thematic import. Proceding in order of increasing complexity and coherence, these comparisons may appear either as correlated multiple strands, as correlated groups of antitheses, or as correlated groups of antitheses governed by a single integrating term.

Turning now from the range of structural possibilities to the poet's actual achievement in individual odes, it will be useful to trace the development of his technique between 1600 and 1628.

1. *A la Reine, sur sa bien-venuë en France* (1600). Malherbe's first completed ode is also his least coherent. Included are five topics — praise, condemnation, sympathetic portrayal, exhortation and prediction. These the poet organized around a single allusive pattern with a conditional inversion. There is no stylistic coherence in this ode, as is immediately apparent from the contradictions that exist in the reference and valuation of related images (e.g., the fire imagery refers both to war and to love, cf. vv. 54 and 164).

2. *Sur l'attentat commis en la personne de sa Majesté le 19 de Décembre 1605* (1606). Vastly richer in matter and more coherent than the first, the second ode consists of four topics — praise, condemnation, exhortation and sympathetic portrayal — all involved in six implicit comparisons: two interlocking allusions (one of which contains a conditional inversion) and four stylistic strands which appear as two correlated sets of antitheses. (The gains in richness and coherence are slightly offset by the awkwardness of this ambitious poem.)

3. *Au feu Roy, sur l'heureux succez du voyage de Sedan* (1606). Free of the awkwardness that mars the second completed ode, the third contains four topics — praise, condemnation, exhortation, and assertions on poetry. The action is modeled on a single allusion containing two inversions. Like the second ode, the third possesses four stylistic strands which appear as two correlated sets of antitheses.

4. *A Monseigneur le Duc de Bellegarde, grand Escuyer de France* (1607-1611). Perhaps plagued with technical difficulties because he was dealing with a lesser nobleman rather than a King or Queen, Malherbe left this ode poorer in matter than any in his canon and less coherent than any but the first; the topics are two — praise and assertions about poetry; there is one allusive pattern containing an inversion and three distinct but correlated stylistic strands.

5. *A la Reine, sur les heureux succez de sa Regence* (1610). By the standards of judgment operative in the present work, this ode must rank as the best that Malherbe composed. It contains all of the literal topics, a single allusion with two implied inversions, and above all six stylistic strands present as three pairs of correlated antitheses governed by the poem's key term.

6. *Pour le Roy, allant chastier la rebellion des Rochelois, et chasser les Anglois, qui en leur faveur estoient descendus en l'isle de Ré* (1628). Again, all topics are present. On the stylistic stratum there are eight strands which form four correlated sets of antitheses. But, despite a local allusion to the Old Testament, indirect reference as such no longer accounts for the poem's total organization.

From the foregoing schemas, it is clear that Malherbe integrated his six completed odes in a definite progression. At first he made use of allusive comparison, while apparently neglecting coherence on the stylistic stratum. Beginning with the second and continuing (with one lapse) until the fifth ode, Malherbe co-ordinated the allusions with ever more tightly knit comparisons of a stylistic origin. In his sixth and last completed ode, he abandoned allusive comparison altogether as a principle of structure, creating instead his largest group of style-based analogies, which appear in fairly close co-ordination with one another.

* * *

That in general these poems possess a remarkable coherence — though varying from one another in kind and degree — justifies their serious reconsideration by those who have seen in them nothing more than a forbidding example of chaste style and lofty sentiments. As this study has shown, Malherbe's dense and paradoxical odes — not unlike the poetry of Racine, Baudelaire, and Valéry — afford a receptive reader the twofold poetic pleasure of recognition and discovery.

APPENDIX:

"Si quelque avorton..."

Begun in 1614, at the outbreak of the "guerre des Princes," the following ode was left unfinished and first appeared in the posthumous 1630 edition of the poet's *Œuvres*. [1]

* * *

POUR LA REINE MERE DU ROY PENDANT SA REGENCE

I   Si quelque avorton de l'envie
     Ose encore lever les yeux,
     Je veux bander contre sa vie
     L'ire de la terre et des cieux;
     Et dans les sçavantes oreilles   5
     Verser de si douces merveilles,
     Que ce miserable corbeau,
     Comm'oiseau d'augure sinistre,
     Banny des rives de Caïstre,
     S'aille cacher dans le tombeau.   10

II   Venez donc, non pas habillées
     Comm'on vous trouve quelquefois,
     En juppe dessous les fueillées

---

[1] Malherbe, II, p. 115.

　　　　　Dansant au silence des bois.
　　　　　Venez en robbes, où l'on voye　　　　　15
　　　　　Dessus les ouvrages de soye
　　　　　Les rayons d'or étinceller;
　　　　　Et chargez de perles vos testes,
　　　　　Comme quand vous allez aux festes
　　　　　Où les Dieux vous font appeller.　　　　20

III　　　Quand le sang boüillant en mes veines
　　　　　Me donnoit de jeunes desirs,
　　　　　Tantost vous souspiriez mes peines,
　　　　　Tantost vous chantiez mes plaisirs;
　　　　　Mais aujourd'huy que mes années　　　25
　　　　　Vers leur fin s'en vont terminées,
　　　　　Sieroit-il bien à mes écris
　　　　　D'ennuyer les races futures
　　　　　Des ridicules avantures
　　　　　D'un amoureux en cheveux gris?　　　　30

IV　　　Non, vierges, non; je me retire
　　　　　De tous ces frivoles discours;
　　　　　Ma Reine est un but à ma lyre
　　　　　Plus juste que nulles amours;
　　　　　Et quand j'auray, comme j'espere,　　35
　　　　　Fait ouïr du Gange à l'Ibere
　　　　　Sa loüange à tout l'univers,
　　　　　Permesse me soit un Cocithe,
　　　　　Si jamais je vous solicite
　　　　　De m'aider à faire des vers.　　　　　40

V　　　　Aussi-bien chanter d'autre chose,
　　　　　Ayant chanté de sa grandeur,
　　　　　Seroit-ce pas aprés la rose
　　　　　Aux pavots chercher de l'odeur?
　　　　　Et des loüanges de la lune　　　　　　45
　　　　　Descendre à la clairté commune
　　　　　D'un de ces feux du firmament,
　　　　　Qui sans profiter et sans nuire,

N'ont receu l'usage de luire
Que par le nombre seulement. 50

VI   Entre les Rois à qui cet âge
Doit son principal ornement,
Ceux de la Tamise et du Tage
Font loüer leur gouvernement;
Mais en de si calmes provinces, 55
Où le peuple adore les Princes,
Et met au degré le plus haut
L'honneur de Sceptre legitime,
Sçauroit-on excuser le crime
De ne regner pas comme il faut? 60

VII   Ce n'est point aux rives d'un fleuve,
Où dorment les vents et les eaux,
Que fait sa veritable preuve
L'art de conduire les vaisseaux;
Il faut en la plaine salée 65
Avoir lutté contre Malée,
Et prés du naufrage dernier
S'estre veu dessous les Pleiades
Eloigné de ports et de rades,
Pour estre creu bon marinier. 70

VIII   Ainsi quand la Grece partie
D'où le mol Anaure couloit,
Traversa les mers de Scithie
En la navire qui parloit,
Pour avoir sceu des Cyanées 75
Tromper les vagues forcenées,
Les pilotes du fils d'Eson,
Dont le nom jamais ne s'efface,
Ont gaigné la premiere place
En la fable de la Toison. 80

IX   Ainsi conservant cet empire
Où l'infidelité du sort
Jointe à la nostre encore pire,

Alloit faire un dernier effort,
Ma Reine acquiert à ses merites 85
Un nom qui n'a point de limites;
Et ternissant le souvenir
Des Reines qui l'ont precedée,
Devient une eternelle idée
De celles qui sont à venir. 90

X   Aussi-tost que le coup tragique
Dont nous fusmes presque abbatus,
Eut fait la fortune publique
L'exercice de ses vertus,
En quelle nouveauté d'orage 95
Ne fut éprouvé son courage?
Et quelles malices de flots,
Par des murmures effroyables,
A des vœux à peine payables
N'obligerent les matelots? 100

XI   Qui n'ouït la voix de Belonne,
Lasse d'un repos de douze ans,
Telle que d'un foudre qui tonne
Appeller tous ses partisans;
Et déja les rages extrémes, 105
Par qui tombent les Diadémes,
Faire apprehender le retour
De ces combats, dont la manie
Est l'eternelle ignominie
De Jarnac et de Moncontour? 110

XII   Qui ne voit encor à cette heure
Tous les infidelles cerveaux
Dont la fortune est la meilleure,
Ne chercher que troubles nouveaux;
Et ressembler à ces fontaines 115
Dont les conduites sousterraines
Passent par un plomb si gasté,
Que tousjours ayant quelque tare,

Au mesme temps qu'on les repare
L'eau s'enfuit d'un autre costé? 120

XIII La paix ne voit rien que menace
De faire renaistre nos pleurs;
Tout s'accorde à nostre bonace;
Les hyvers nous donnent des fleurs;
Et si les pasles Eumenides, 125
Pour réveiller nos parricides,
Toutes trois ne sortent d'enfer,
Le repos du siecle où nous sommes
Va faire à la moitié des hommes
Ignorer que c'est que le fer. 130

XIV Themis, capitale ennemie
Des ennemis de leur devoir,
Comme un rocher est affermie
En son redoutable pouvoir;
Elle va d'un pas et d'un ordre, 135
Où la censure n'a que mordre;
Et les loix qui n'exceptent rien
De leur glaive et de leur balance,
Font tout perdre à la violance
Qui veut avoir plus que le sien. 140

XV Nos champs mesme ont leur abondance
Hors de l'outrage des voleurs;
Les festins, les jeux, et la dance,
En bannissent toutes douleurs.
Rien n'y gemit, rien n'y souspire; 145
Chaque Amarille a son Tytire,
Et sous l'épaisseur des rameaux,
Il n'est place où l'ombre soit bonne,
Qui soir et matin ne resonne
Ou de voix, ou de chalumeaux. 150

XVI Puis, quand ces deux grands Hymenées,
Dont le fatal embrassement

Doit applanir les Pyrenées,
Auront leur accomplissement,
Devons-nous douter qu'on ne voye, 155
Pour accompagner cette joye,
L'encens germer en nos buissons,
La myrrhe couler en nos ruës,
Et sans l'usage des charruës
Nos plaines jaunir de moissons? 160

XVII Quelle moins hautaine esperance
Pouvons-nous concevoir alors,
Que de conquester à la France
La Propontide en ses deux bors?
Et vengeant de succez prosperes 165
Les infortunes de nos peres
Que tient l'Egypte ensevelis,
Aller si prés du bout du monde,
Que le soleil sorte de l'onde
Sur la terre des fleurs de lys? 170

XVIII Certes ces miracles visibles
Excedant le penser humain,
Ne sont point ouvrages possibles
A moins qu'une immortelle main.
Et la raison ne se peut dire, 175
De nous voir en nostre navire
A si bon port acheminez,
Ou sans fard et sans flatterie,
C'est Pallas que cette Marie,
Par qui nous sommes gouvernez. 180

XIX Quoy qu'elle soit, Nymphe ou Déesse,
De sang immortel ou mortel,
Il faut que le monde confesse
Qu'il ne vit jamais rien de tel;
Et quiconque fera l'histoire 185
De ce grand chef-d'œuvre de gloire,
L'incredule posterité
Rejettera son témoignage,

APPENDIX

   S'il ne la dépeint belle, et sage,
   Au deça de la verité.   190

XX Grand Henry, grand foudre de guerre,
   Que cependant que parmy nous
   Ta valeur étonnoit la terre,
   Les Destins firent son espous;
   Roy dont la memoire est sans blasme,   195
   Que dis-tu de cette belle ame,
   Quand tu la vois si dignement
   Adoucir toutes nos absynthes,
   Et se tirer des labyrinthes
   Où la met ton éloignement?   200

XXI Que dis-tu lors que tu remarques
   Aprés ses pas ton heritier,
   De la sagesse des Monarques
   Monter le penible sentier?
   Et pour étendre sa Couronne,   205
   Croistre comme un fan de lyonne?
   Que s'il peut un jour égaler
   Sa force avecques sa furie,
   Les Nomades n'ont bergerie,
   Qu'il ne suffise à desoler.   210

XXII Qui doute que si de ses armes
   Ilion avoit eu l'appuy,
   Le jeune Atride avecque larmes
   Ne s'en fust retourné chez luy;
   Et qu'aux beaux champs de la Phrygie, 215
   De tant de batailles rougie,
   Ne fussent encor honorez
   Ces ouvrages des mains celestes,
   Que jusques à leurs derniers restes
   La flamme Grecque a devorez?[2]   220

       ✿ ✿ ✿

---

[2] Malherbe, I, pp. 210-217.

Technical explanations for Malherbe's abandonment of this ode have varied significantly from one critic to another. Before the presentation of our opinion, a review of the two most influential theories will be useful.

For Professor Wadsworth, "the poet's artistic scruples prevented his finishing a work which he found irremediably defective." The evidence for this emerges from the order and articulation of themes:

> Stanzas 1-5. Complex introduction. Violent denunciation of some enemy whom the poet will overpower with his verse (1). Invocation to the Muses, but not for love poetry; he has grown old and gray (2-3). Only the Queen is worthy of his art (4-5). 6-9. Praise for the Queen as a great pilot of the ship of state. 10-12. The rebellion and its dangers. 13-15. May France's peace and property continue. 16-17. The forthcoming royal marriages will strengthen France and lead to further conquests. 18-19. But a good helmsman is needed; praise for Marie. 20-22. Invocation to the shades of Henri IV. Don't you admire your Queen (20) and the progress of your son (21)? Such a prince could have saved Troy from destruction (22). [3]

In his critique, Professor Wadsworth points out that the "first two surviving stanzas contain obscurities which indicate that something was intended to precede them." Moreover, "there is a rupture in the continuity of the poem between stanzas 12 and 13; after saying that France is in grave danger because of the rebellious princes, Malherbe proclaims that France is enjoying an era of blissful peace." As for the finale, "this last stanza, although emphatic and resounding, presents a side issue and does not form an appropriate ending for the ode." In the body of the poem, "one is struck by the abrupt, unprepared shifts from topic to topic and above all by the extreme multiplicity of themes... [there] would seem to be too many components to piece together in a poem in honor of a single person, the Queen." [4] In short, the abortive ode embodies every defect of logical exposition that Malherbe had almost overcome in his third, fourth, and fifth odes: discontinuity, irrelevancy, and uncertain emphasis.

---

[3] Wadsworth, pp. 193-194.
[4] Wadsworth, p. 194.

APPENDIX 121

To Professor Fromilhague, the poet abandoned this ode because of a significant change in his theory and practice of versification:

> C'est probablement entre 1615 et 1620 que Maynard et Malherbe édictent la nécessité d'un arrêt au septième vers du dizain (cf. R. Fromilhague, *Malherbe, technique et création poétique,* pp. 436-437). Or, dans cette ode, huit strophes seulement, sur vingt-deux, suivent la règle. Presque toute la pièce était donc à refaire, et le poète a reculé devant l'entreprise.[5]

The preceding arguments are very compelling. To them may be added the further observation that in this ode, the comparative structures by which Malherbe had assured the coherence of his other odes are meager and imperfectly developed. First, the ode neither recapitulates nor contains variations on the unparticularized motifs of any mythic or legendary pattern, including ones to which the poet incidentally refers while praising the Queen, e. g. those of Jason and Theseus (see stanzas VIII and XX). Equally important is the fact that the poem's style presents irreconciliable contradictions. Two examples will suffice to demonstrate this point. First, Malherbe united light with the nobility of the Muses who are to come

> ... en robbes, où l'on voye
> Dessus les ouvrages de soye
> Les rayons d'or étinceller.   (vv. 15-17)

The poet also linked light with the Queen herself, who is "ce grand chef-d'œuvre de gloire" (l. 186). But light is also associated with evil: "la flamme Grecque" (l. 220), for example, which would not have destroyed Troy, had the Dauphin been present. With respect to space, Malherbe makes his customary distinction between those entities which by nature are or should be elevated, e. g. the Queen, whose special trait is "grandeur" (v. 42), and those, such as the unnamed enemy mentioned in the first stanza, who, the poet wishes, "s'aille cacher dans le tombeau" (v. 10). But

---

[5] Malherbe, II, p. 115.

Malherbe also compares that very enemy a to a "miserable corbeau" (v. 7), which by its nature soars and flies.

This failure to achieve metaphorical coherence may be one of the reasons for Malherbe's abandonment of the ode: having previously perfected a formula which interwove plot and character, thought and style, the poet may have insisted on repeating the process here or withholding from the public a poem lacking in "higher hidden order." It seems equally probable, however, that the ode's incipient stylistic coherence would have developed more fully in successive revisions which, because of the insoluble problems outlined by Professors Wadsworth and Fromilhague, the poet simply did not undertake.

SELECTIVE BIBLIOGRAPHY

1. *Text.*

   MALHERBE, FRANÇOIS DE. *Œuvres poétiques.* 2 vols. Eds. René Fromilhague and Raymond Lebègue. Paris: Société Les Belles Lettres, 1968.

2. *On Malherbe and the Literature of His Time.*

   BRAY, RENÉ. *La Formation de la doctrine classique en France.* 2nd ed. Paris: Nizet, 1957.

   BRUNOT, FERDINAND. *La Doctrine de Malherbe d'après son commentaire sur Desportes.* Paris: Masson, 1891.

   FROMILHAGUE, RENÉ. *Malherbe: technique et création poétique.* Paris: Colin, 1954.

   ———. *La Vie de Malherbe: apprentissage et luttes* (1555-1610). Paris: Colin, 1954.

   GREEN, MARIA A. *Sovereign Power and Sovereign Glory: A Study of the Influence of Jean Bodin's Political Ideas on Malherbe.* Unpublished Ph.D. dissertation, University of Washington, 1969.

   LANSON, GUSTAVE. *Histoire de la littérature française.* Paris: Hachette, 1912.

   LEBEGUE, RAYMOND. *La Poésie française de 1560 à 1630.* 2 vols. Paris: Société d'Edition d'Enseignement Supérieur, 1951.

   ROUSSET, JEAN. *La littérature de l'âge baroque en France.* Paris: José Corti, 1953.

   ———. *L'Intérieur et l'extérieur.* Paris: José Corti, 1968.

   ———. "La Poésie au temps de Malherbe: la métaphore," *Dix-septième Siècle,* No. 31 (April, 1956), 353-370.

   WADSWORTH, PHILIP A. "Form and Content in the Odes of Malherbe," *Publications of the Modern Language Association,* 78 (June, 1963), 190-195.

   WINEGARTEN, RENÉE. *French Lyric Poetry in the Age of Malherbe.* Manchester: Manchester University Press, 1954.

3. *Esthetics and Method.*

   BROOKS, CLEANTH. *The Well-Wrought Urn.* New York: Harcourt, Brace, 1947.

CRANE, RONALD S. *The Languages of Criticism and the Structure of Poetry*. Toronto: University of Toronto Press, 1953.
HUBERT, JUDD D. *Essai d'exégèse racinienne*. Paris: Nizet, 1956.
———. *Molière and the Comedy of the Intellect*. Berkeley and Los Angeles: University of California Press, 1962.
PASCO, A. H. "Marcel, Albertine and Balbec in Proust's Allusive Complex," *Romanic Review*, 62 (1971), 113-126.
PEPPER, STEPHEN C. *The Basis of Criticism in the Arts*. Cambridge: Harvard University Press, 1945.
———. *World Hypotheses*. Berkeley: University of California Press, 1942.
PROPP, VLADIMIR. *The Morphology of the Folktale*. Translated by Laurence Scott. 2nd. ed., revised by Louis A. Wagner. Austin: The University of Texas Press, 1968.
WEINBERG, BERNARD. *The Art of Jean Racine*. Chicago: University of Chicago Press, 1963.
———. *The Limits of Symbolism*. Chicago: University of Chicago Press, 1967.
WELLEK, RENÉ AND AUSTIN WARREN. *Theory of Literature*. New York: Harcourt, Brace, 1949.
WIMSATT, W. K. *The Verbal Icon*. Lexington: University of Kentucky Press, 1954.

www.ingramcontent.com/pod-product-compliance
Lightning Source LLC
Chambersburg PA
CBHW020420230426
43663CB00007BA/1250